The seventh at The European Club is regarded as one of the World's 100 Greatest Golf Holes.

The tone of the round is set at the very first hole as those bunkers say hello.

Fifty Years In A Bunker

The Creation of A World Top-100 Golf Links
at
THE EUROPEAN CLUB

Pat Ruddy

with photography by

Gerard Ruddy

First published in 2007
by the
RUDDY GOLF LIBRARY
The European Club
Brittas Bay
County Wicklow
Ireland
info@theeuropeanclub.com

ISBN 978-0-9556049-0-4
© Copyright Pat Ruddy

Printed In Hong Kong
Front-cover - Hole eleven at The European Club

For my wife, Bernardine, who is the most patient of people.

In memory of my parents, Sid and Moya, who introduced
me to golf and to all good things.

Saluting our children who have endured long hours and trying
moments in the creation of The European Club. Take a
bow - Gerard, Bernardine Jnr, twins Sidon and
Patrick, and baby Zilla.

The third hole tumbles downhill into the dunes.

Preface

There was a time when only old fellows got to write a book about their fifty years in golf.
Fellows like Horace Hutchinson, Andrew Kirkaldy and Bernard Darwin.
Amazingly, while still quite young, my turn has arrived!

It is difficult to accept that fifty years have flown by since the thought of creating and owning a golf place of one's own presented itself to a young mind.

Now the deed has been done and at a level beyond youthful imagination as the links at The European Club has been voted into the World's Top-100 Golf Courses and golfers from all over the world, including many of the greatest players of all-time such as my particular hero Johnny Miller and Tiger Woods, come to play it.

The only pity is that my parents, Sid and Moya, did not live to share the day. They would have been shocked and thrilled. Their ghosts, and those of a great many lovely golfing friends who have shuffled off this mortal fairway during one's life, linger out there in the dunes and form a real presence when one takes time for solitary practice sessions after the golfers are gone and the sun is setting.

It has come as a shock to the nervous system that one's golfing place has been chosen to host the various national championships. There were the Irish Ladies' Amateur Championships in 2001 and in 2006; the Irish Men's Amateur Close Championship in 2006; and the Irish Professional Close Championship in 2007. No higher honour can be bestowed on a golf links than that of hosting the national championships of one's country and one is humbly grateful for being trusted so.

It has been a miraculous journey since the thought of creating a golfing corner of one's own first occurred away back in 1957! How it was achieved is difficult to explain.

It seems that destiny has much to do with what passes for success in this life. The impossible putts drop for the champions while they lip out for others. One man is granted a long life while another is afflicted with unthinkable suffering. Luck plays such a big part in our lives that it is silly to seek credit for all that happens. All that one does is subdue fear, take the opportunities when they present themselves and play the ball as it lies. Sometimes, if you want something badly enough it will happen!

Chances have had to be taken. There are financial risks associated with a project as large as the creation of a major golf links. To have overcome them from the base of income of a golf-writer with further earnings from golf architecture is quite amazing. The caution and modesty of a man of the land, keeping expenditure within one's means and patiently taking criticism from those who expected one to run when one could only walk, proved a major asset.

While others were building golf businesses one was intent only on creating a place for one's own golf where friends would be made welcome. There was no need for ornamentation and excess. The constant thought has been that there are centuries of life ahead for The European Club and it will grow and grow long after one is gone providing it is started on a sound footing.

Creating a golf place for oneself is an exciting and rewarding exercise. It becomes a matter for stress when that place transforms itself from a simple duckling into an elegant swan and the experts start to pass judgement. Instead of playing one's game quietly in a closely-mown field behind high hedges, which would have been satisfactory, one is caught in the glare of international publicity and can but ask commentators to consider that one has given it his best shot and hopes that the same blessings will be bestowed on them starting with an enjoyable round of golf at lovely Brittas Bay.

PAT RUDDY

The European Club
May 2007

The seventeenth hole plunges into a valley in the dunes and settles many matches.

HOW IT BEGAN

The genesis of a golfer's dream

The road to the links of The European Club was a very long one. Forty years long and criss-crossing Ireland and much of the golfing world.

The idea of having a golf course of one's own arose in the late 1950s when word came through from Texas that Jack Burke and Jimmy Demaret were creating a course of their own and calling it The Champions Club.

What a great idea and what a wonderful name!

Kids have a grand way of seeing the possibilities without being distracted by practicalities. So it was that the dream of having a course of one's own took shape, without a thought to matters of finance, and it would have to be a grand course. A champion course by another name!

It didn't matter that golf course ownership was hardly known in the Ireland of the 1960s. Almost every course was controlled by co-operative clubs and the profit motive and real estate development hadn't entered the equation.

It didn't matter that golf course ownership wasn't seen as a business proposition back then. Commerce didn't enter the thought process. It was to be golf for golf's sake. It was about the freedom to shape a golf course of one's own and unlimited freedom to go play on it. A simple thought.

Slowly the pieces fell into place. A career as a golf-writer, then as a golf course designer and as a promoter of golf events all proved to be significant preparation for the big project. It wasn't obvious at the time but, looking back, it seems that the hand of destiny was at work. Getting to know the wider golfing world, getting to know what was out there, was an essential first move.

The life of a golf-writer is truly blessed. It brings one to the nicest places, to the big events and into contact with the legions of nice people who play and organise the game. It may be work, it may not be a great station for a nervous person who dislikes panic deadlines or for somebody seeking a regular pattern to life week-after-week, but it is a glorious and noble pursuit and it helped a normal person to travel the world just like the millionaires of old and to mingle with the millionaires of today.

To get paid for doing so much of what one likes to do is remarkably nice. To get to build a golf course of one's own on such meagre wages was to prove even more remarkable.

The job brought one to places which had been read about as a boy and opportunities arose to play the great courses. First came all the classic links of Ireland. Places like Portmarnock, Royal Dublin, The Island, County Louth, Royal County Down, Royal Portrush, remote Rosapenna and Portsalon, one's beloved home links at County Sligo, Lahinch and Ballybunion. Rain or shine it didn't matter. The score didn't matter. These were enchanted lands and enraptured days.

The Open Championship, in particular, and other tournaments lured one to the great fairways in Britain and very soon every dune and every bunker and swale on the classics over there was as familiar and explored as every nook and cranny of the Irish links. The great British links were played and the great players watched in competitive action on them. Bobby Locke and Peter Thomson, the young Gary Player, Arnold Palmer and Jack Nicklaus, my heroes Johnny Miller and Lee Trevino! They performed wondrous deeds and one thrilled at it all and was instinctively learning all the while.

Of course, America had to be seen, savoured and studied. But the budgets at Irish newspapers didn't allow for such far flung adventures at that time and there was nothing for it but to resign and go freelance. Time to contribute stories to magazines and newspapers in many countries and launch a new golf magazine, the Golfer's Companion, in 1972. Now, the golfing world was one's oyster subject to flying mostly economy and being content with modest lodgings.

What a place is America! Great golf from coast-to-coast! Two or three prolonged visits annually brought into focus great courses such as Augusta, Winged Foot, Oakland Hills, Oakmont, Shinnecock Hills, Pine Valley, Lake Nona and Seminole in Florida, Peachtree, the great desert courses in Arizona and Nevada, Pinehurst, the Californian greats at Pebble Beach, Cypress Point and San Francisco, and Arnold Palmer hosting the Ryder Cup at Laurel Valley.

The senses were battered with new shapes and hues and sounds. Waterfalls and fountains, entrance gates that screamed importance, palatial clubhouses with people to park your car and clean your shoes, fairways that were like carpets and heaving greens with the early creeping bent covers that looked great and played even better.

All of it was enjoyed and much of it was assimilated into the inner being. This, from Ireland to Monterey, was golf!

Amid all this one became aware that Augusta is very special. This is the hot house, the central laboratory, of golf course architecture. A place where they submit their course to the most searching test by the best players in the world each April and then review and debate and make some improvements. It became a study watching them move. Sometimes the changes were as subtle as a lip added to the bunker at the right of the sixteenth green after Billy Casper had the audacity to use a putter out of it the previous year. More recently the improvements have been on the grander scale as technology and physical training have transformed the way the game is played.

Tees and trees have been added. Angles have been changed just enough to matter. Bunkers have moved. The greens have become faster, maybe too fast at times, and a little rough has been grown. The message to an enquiring mind, one aiming at creating its own golfing home, was quite clear. A golf course has to be a living thing. It has to move with the game and with the developing intelligence of those who control it. To stand still is to become outdated. So, the resolve was to create as good a golf links as one could and then, working steadfastly year after year, continue to improve it and ensure that it evolves with the game itself. Just two decades have been devoted to the task so far at The European Club and every day continues to be intellectually stimulating as multitudes of exciting ideas clamber for attention and activation.

Meanwhile, another big lesson was learned from Charles Yates who proved to be the perfect American gentleman in making one welcome to The Masters. Year after year the lovely letters of invitation came and Charles Yates, until time took its inevitable toll and he retired only when he couldn't physically go on enjoying and helping the game and the club he loved, was always there and displaying an astounding ability to make everyone feel like a billion dollars. He would be deep in concentrated talk with important players and important people when we arrived but he would break away from them to greet his Irish friends and make it clear that they were welcome and a part of the scene.

An astounding performance by a great champion and contemporary and friend of Bobby Jones. All the more impressive because it wasn't a performance at all but natural goodness and awareness for other people's feelings. A great and admirable man and an inspiration to anyone wishing to share the happiness of golf with others. If just a tiny percentage of that magical American charm could be learned and made a part of the culture at The European Club!

A further lesson was absorbed at the 1986 U.S. Open at Shinnecock Hills when our enthusiastic host Jim Lynch insisted on everyone being out of bed before dawn and over to the club to help get the course ready for play. Just one of the tasks was to brush the heavy dew off those pristine fairways and be gone from sight and from sound before the first players teed-off. So that is how it is done!

The decision was made not to have dew covered greens at The European Club when the players arrived, ever, and to see how close an Irish links could get to the perfection of those fairways. Why not try, on a day to day basis, to give our golfers a little taste of the service which is lavished upon the top tournament players at championship time?

It takes that extra bit of effort having the crew out before play each day and getting the machine noise out the back-nine before play begins. To allow this preparation to take place is why we start our first game as late as 8a.m. daily. Even at that there can be problems to address as all too often the first game of the day is a single player, or a twosome, intent on galloping around the links at record speed and stampeding the grounds crew in the process. Sometimes, the crew has to skip a hole and then comeback behind the galloping golfers to finish a task or two.

Everywhere one visited over three decades of intense travel drew attention to how hard the best places work at presenting the best possible golf in beautiful condition, at presenting comfortable off-course facilities, and to the almost unfailing (there will always be exceptions) courtesy and friendship of golfers towards each other.

To have seen so many great golf courses, to have seen the great champions of almost five decades play great championships on them, to have played most of them, to have photographed all of them and to have been wined and dined at all of them ... has added a wealth of images and information to the data base of a mind that always has been preoccupied with such matters.

All of these images and memories, together with happy memories of the simpler golf age of the 1950s, have been distilled and mulled over during the first twenty years of development of the links at The European Club as the effort continues to make the links better and better.

The plan is to continue this effort for years to come. There is always so much to be done when one strives to earn a place amongst the best in any field of activity. Meanwhile, it is extremely rewarding to find most golfers enjoying the experience of playing at The European Club and even those who score higher than they would wish acknowledging that they have been in a first-class contest with nature and with golf design and that the best rewards are those which have to be earned.

THIRD TIME LUCKY

A helicopter ride reveals much.

All the golfing, all the writing, all the travelling to see great players competing and all the visits to the world's most magnificent golf clubs formed part of an inexorable trek towards The European Club.

A golf place of one's own was going to happen one day. For years, even to this day, every handsome field that drifted past the window of train or car was evaluated speedily for its golf potential. A lovely greensite here. Over there - what a magnificent tree to turn a fairway! A tee on that hill would provide a marvellous downhill drive. Such dreams aren't just visited at odd moments; they are present and possessive even when awake in a dark room at night and waiting for sleep to return.

Inevitably, there would be false starts and disappointments along the way. It was a case of third time lucky when one got started at The European Club.

One's first attempt to establish a golf course of one's own happened in the mid-1970s when limited funding was allied to the instinct of the homing pigeon. A poor parcel of land was acquired in south County Sligo, where many happy boyhood days had been spent, largely because property prices were lowest in that part of Ireland and because there was that added comfort factor of coming home. Mistake and mistake!

The lessons to be learned were that golf is best created where the land is golfing land, where there is a demand for golf, and where drainage is a positive rather than a negative. Golf is best when the ball does not plug to its axis and the golf shoe remains dry and clean.

The drainage lesson came in two parts. First, wondering why everyone else was so lacking in imagination when locating their buildings fairly close to a public road rather than going for a lovely raised site further into the land, one chose a hilltop about 800-yards from the road and began to build

The eighth hole is a beautiful dog-leg right named in honour of Fred Daly.

an access road to the clubhouse of the future. Months, and many thousands of lost pounds later, the lesson had been learned. Truck after truck of stone was simply sucked down by the marshy ground and every yard gained cost a fortune.

Before that lesson was fully absorbed, and before one could consider a Plan B for clubhouse location, a very dramatic event caused the entire project to be abandoned.

A large mobile home had served as the work base and living quarters through the Summer. A devoted wife, with four children aged under eight to mind, joined in the work. Monday through wednesday was spent on the site, working the fields by day and talking and sleeping in that mobile home by night, and on thursday through sunday we were back at home to keep our publishing enterprise moving, or a tournament had to be attended, or a visit had to be made to a golf course one had under construction for someone else. It is exhausting to look back at now and one can only wonder at the stupidity, the tenacity and the dedication of youth.

There were many challenging moments like the day when one of our brand new tractors went missing. It took three days of driving around in ever increasing circles to find it parked outside a farmhouse ten miles away. The resulting conversation with the farmer is worth recording:-

"I think that is my tractor out in your yard?" Reply- "Could be, I borrowed it."

"I would like you to leave it back now." Reply: "I'm not finished with it yet."

With a little persuasion he left it back real fast! And the work went on.

Grass was mown and flags were placed on the sites of greens to be. It was great! The mobile home was located on a hill where the future clubhouse was to go so that the "course" could be admired from its windows. That was a lucky move because came a morning we awoke to find that the Owenmore River had burst its banks and flooded everything for 360-degrees around us and we were on the only bit of land above water.

We were now the proud owners of a lake! The golf flags waved gently above the waters in the places we had planned elevated greens. Others were gone, presumably on their way to the Atlantic, and we had to sit tight for three days before the flood receded enough to allow us to exit the property and the dream. It seemed that operation golf course was finished. But the golfing mind would not let go.

Very soon we were travelling up and down the country two or three days a week looking at possible locations for a new beginning. Dozens of properties were evaluated before we came upon a most tempting proposition at Lough Rynn Castle in County Leitrim.

18

The Clements family, the Lords Leitrim, had just recently ceased to live here after centuries of lavishing love and money on the place. They left a lovely castle, a magnificent walled garden, a saw mill, a coach house, a folly and about 400-acres of mostly lake and some land. It was beguiling. It was a veritable small town in which one could establish a publishing works and other enterprises while playing golf and living like a lord in a castle!

The estate was rundown. It had extended to over 2,500-acres at one stage, with a further 52,000 acres in Donegal and more properties in Kildare and London, but the Land Commission had intervened and caused most of the Lough Rynn lands to be redistributed in small holdings to local people. The sane side of the mind, the part that recalled the Sligo flood, was not happy with the lake and with the heavy nature of dozens of low-lying acres. The fact that the access roads were long and in great need of costly repairs resonated as memories of the other costly mistake in Sligo. It was an inviting but nervous moment.

A price was agreed. A golf course was outlined. The solicitors were at work. Then, just in time, caution prevailed and we retreated. Besides the technical problems, there was no local demand for golf around Lough Rynn Castle and tourism golf was only beginning so it was highly unlikely that people would flock from all over the world to play there and help a workable budget to be created. It was best to wait for a better proposition.

Interestingly, a golf enterprise got underway in Lough Rynn some twenty years later. A local developer converted the castle into a lovely hotel, built housing in the grounds and engaged Nick Faldo to design a golf course which was under construction at time of writing this volume. It seems that we may yet enjoy a night's sleep in "our castle" and play golf in the grounds!

The Lough Rynn episode was to prove just one's first contact with the legend of the Lords Leitrim as the opportunity arose to design some significant golf holes in the extensive sand dunes at Rosapenna, in north-Donegal, in the 1990s and early-2000s. One of the Lords had invited Old Tom Morris over there in the 1890s to advise on the establishment of a golf resort which was to rank as one of the finest in the world until going into decline through the ravages of two world wars and the shift of holiday activity from the coasts of Scotland and Ireland to the Mediterranean and further afield.

It was quite a thrill to be invited onto a design ticket alongside Old Tom, Harry Vardon and James Braid. A brand new 18-hole links, now known as Sandy Hills, was the first Rosapenna project, and then one did some sensitive improvements to the lovely but dated Old Tom front-nine in the broad valley nearest to the Atlantic. Finally, one persuaded Frank Casey, the owner of Rosapenna, that a new nine holes could be created in a remaining patch of dunesland and that this would allow the abandonment of the mundane upland holes of the back-nine which were out of character to begin with and were damaged by the intrusion of housing. Thus, Rosapenna was brought back to a positive position in the modern golfing world and one knows that Lord Leitrim and Old Tom would approve.

Meantime, The European Club was underway thanks to an amazing breakthrough at Ballybunion. We had the contract to publish the yearbook of the Golfing Union of Ireland in the early-1980s and part of the agreement was that the front-cover illustration would be politically neutralised by featuring only a picture of the clubhouse from the venue of that year's Irish Amateur Close Championship. Came the turn of Ballybunion and their clubhouse of the time, while sound and practical, did not present a pretty picture for a front-cover.

We offered to rent a helicopter and take some aerial shots of Ballybunion with the clubhouse included but faded into the background. We would not depart from the essence of our agreement but we would get an attractive cover illustration. Permission was given and a revelation followed.

As the helicopter made its way from Shannon along the coast to Ballybunion it became clear that marsh and meadow abounded and sand dunes were in scarce supply. Then, up on the horizon rose the dunes at Ballybunion like a great reverse oasis. Whereas adventurers were known to stagger from the desert towards a green oasis we were going from emerald fields into sand dunes! It was a shock to the senses and prompted the immediate thought that a helicopter survey of the Irish coastline would reveal any remaining sand dune sites suitable for the establishment of a golf links!

This was a critical decision. The emphasis moved from seeking to establish a golf course to establishing a golf links. How a person who had spent most of his childhood playing on links didn't think clearly on this issue from the start remains a mystery today. It was almost a calamitous mistake but fate had intervened.

Now, a links is the cream when it comes to golf. It is the original of the species and where the game began on sandy terrain along the sea. The dry going allows the game to be played in great comfort all year through and the combination of fast running ground, tall roughs and fine-grassed fairways and greens is quite intoxicating when taken together with the turbulent topographical heaves and the capricious nature of the winds that are, in turn, at their most baleful and most soothing where there is a conjunction of land, sea and air.

The term linksland needs definition here as it creates a good deal of confusion in the modern world. A confusion exacerbated greatly by the promoters of clifftop courses and pushed-up farmland near the sea and by the owners of featureless inland tracts who seek to enhance their prospects by describing their creations as "linkslike" rather than barren and devoid of character. They have to know that they are selling a line and it is sad when those who should know better lend their names to the deceit.

A true links can happen only on true linksland; ie, on the sandy deposit left by the oceans as they receded, or blown up by the winds from the beaches, and which "links" the seashore to the fertile inland soils. So, the golfers went to the links to play golf and through time people began to talk about golf links.

In fact, true links is a rarity with little more than 170 of them in existence and very few more are likely to happen due to environmental politics. So, less than 0.5% of the world's golf facilities are links and, taking into account their age profile and the scant number of golfing years left to many of them, only a tiny fraction of the world's golfers could hope to get even one game on any one links if they were all to queue-up for the rest of their lives for the privilige of getting just one such links experience each! That is amazing but true. As the world's golf population continues to grow and multiply , and the number of links does not grow very much (if at all), the linksland golf game will become even more precious and treasured.

All of these thoughts crystallised after the helicopter journey to Ballybunion. To the links we must go. In view of the Ballybunion experience there was nothing for it but to conduct an aerial survey of the Irish coastline. The mission was to identify any remaining sites suitable for the establishment of a major new golf links.

Several days were devoted to the helicopter search. It produced startling results. Astonishingly, there was a lovely tract of sand dunes lying idle on the Irish Sea only thirty-five miles south of Dublin. It was ear-marked as the first choice if it could be acquired and, as fate would have it, the opportunity arose within two years.

The property came on the market in 1986 and all the stops were pulled-out to buy it. It was one of those situations where there seemed to be an external force driving things along and one was merely the instrument through which it would happen.

A great adventure began to unfold with plenty of ups and downs on the road ahead but also the reward of a place amongst the World's Top-100 Golf Courses.

MIRACLES DO HAPPEN

After years of effort the game is on.

With about a mile of frontage onto the Irish Sea this was a property to die for. The dunes ran inland for about half-a-mile and allowed holes to be planned in every direction on the compass to ensure maximum engagement with variations of wind and light. There were sandhills as high as eighty feet and valleys as deep as forty feet to give great movement and depth to the links. A perfect site upon which to attempt a golf masterpiece.

It was perfect in another way, too. It was close to the capital city and yet far enough out to enjoy the tranquillity of the ages. Since then it has got a lot closer to the city with the creation of a European highway all the way down the east coast of Ireland, from Belfast to Rosslare, bypassing Dublin along the way. Suddenly, all the main seaports and Dublin International Airport were within easy reach and the city was only 40-minutes away.

It was on the same side of the city as our home and publishing business, within easy reach to facilitate comfortable management of all factors, and it was right in the centre of the biggest concentration of golfers in Ireland meaning that we should have a local support base as well as a touring golfer interface. This is a great help to a golf project and especially in a place where the game is played all year. We could effectively hope for a vibrant tourist season and strong enough localised Winter activity to make it worthwhile keeping the lights on. So, it has come to pass that we played some golf on all but two days in the first fourteen years of play!

A favourable microclimate has allowed this to happen. We enjoy what one would describe as a great GOLF CLIMATE. Very often, golf is played at at The European Club even as those just ten miles away are frost bound or enduring heavy rainfall.

The fifteenth green sits on the edge of Mizen Head and commands magnificent views of the links and the Irish Sea.

The official meteorological records for Ireland show that we have averaged just over half the annual rainfall that places like Ballybunion and Lahinch on the Atlantic coast have had since 1950, an average of 988mm per annum to their 1,600mm. But we get only about one-fifth of their GOLF RAIN as forecasts regularly show a repetitive pattern of rain arriving in from the Atlantic in the morning, just as they prepare to go golfing in the west, and arriving with us on the east coast at nighfall just as we finish playing!

So it is that one appeals against the stereotype image of a damp Ireland being imposed on The European Club. We are located in the sunny southeast and find it difficult to accept criticisms of our weather, save on exceptional occasions, from those whose home courses are closed in Winter by snow and frost, uncomfortable to play in Summer through excessive heat, populated by crocodiles and snakes (of which we have none) and subject to the occasional hurricane or tornado!

Despite these advantages the task had to be approached with respect. Buying land, building a golf course, developing a clubhouse and financing the entire to maturity entails a lot of money. This is true on a relative scale in any age. It is not an exercise for the foolish and quite a few people have discovered this as they have over-estimated the ability of golf to finance huge borrowings.

The first thing was to acquire the land. We had some funds saved over the years, including the proceeds of the sale of the Sligo lands, and a good credit rating. But, as the sale came to our attention fairly late in the day it was a scramble to talk to banks. So it was that in the hour before the auction the commercial bank proved a little less than helpful when promising a decision on our borrowing requirement the next day! All they could say was that it should be okay.

There was nothing for it but to go ahead and buy the land anyway knowing that everything was predestined including the finance. The bank came-up trumps next day.

Then the miracles started to happen. Irish golf tourism had a major problem at that time insofar as all but a few of the big attraction golf courses were under the control of co-operatives of members and when the members came out to play at weekends the tourists could not get a game. In this situation it was impossible to market Ireland as a reliable all-week golfing destination.

The new grants changed all that and helped to stimulate the already growing interest in golf course development. It was quite amazing how so many farmers, accountants and non-golfers started to build courses precisely when we got going after almost thirty years of dreaming and trying!

Some forty of these projects, including all the high profile places like The K-Club and Mount Juliet,

The fourth hole is a big par-4 uphill and it commands great respect.

received grants of varying sizes and we got one, too, and it helped a bit to speed the project on its way. It was good to see golf get government support like any other creator of employment and wealth.

In return for the grant we undertook to welcome tourist golfers for at least ten years after opening. This was no problem as we had never planned to be other than welcoming of a controlled volume of visitors, never taking so many as to make the golf uncomfortably crowded, in the great tradition of Irish hospitality. After all, part of the fun of the game is meeting golf enthusiasts from other places and exchanging stories.

The next miracle emerged within weeks when the new European Highway down the east coast was announced. At the start, the journey from Dublin to The European Club could take anything up to two hours as it involved working along winding roads and through varied traffic jams in the towns of Bray, Newtownmountkennedy, Ashford and Rathnew. The new highway has by-passed all of these and, further north, Dublin itself giving a guaranteed 45-minute journey into Dublin and moving us within easy time reach of Portmarnock and Royal County Down. An amazing development which could not have been foreseen in the Ireland of the 1980s.

The sudden and huge upsurge in golf course development provided the third major miracle. The legendary Eddie Hackett, a great hero of mine, and I were the only two regular practitioners of course design within Ireland through the 1970s and it is fair to say that we worked for peanuts, whenever we were paid. Now there was a Golf Rush akin to the days of the Gold Rush in olden days in America. Suddenly, there was work aplenty and money to be made from design projects just at a time that one needed money like never before!

The most significant breakthrough came just about that time when two men called to our home and asked a simple question: How do you make money out of golf? Come in and let's talk, was the response. Several cups of tea later and Hugo Flinn, Joe Cowhie and I had started a friendship which would last for many years and see us work together on the development of St. Margaret's Golf Club near Dublin Airport followed by the splendid Druid's Glen and Druid's Heath courses not far from The European Club. The Druids development was especially important as Hugo Flinn, who lives nearby, accepted my observation that the big boom in golf development was centred mostly to the north and west of Dublin and that I was largely home alone in County Wicklow to the south. It could only make sense to have a friendly neighbour to help attract golfers to that side of town.

We have been happy and mutually supportive neighbours ever since and it is a joy to watch their two courses and our own links mature with each passing year. Golf courses are like that. They get better with age while we humans gently fade away and have to content ourselves with the thought that our golfing footprints will last and give pleasure long after we are gone.

The now meaningful cash flows from course design work helped get things moving along at The European Club. But it was still a big financial challenge as five further costly land transactions had to be made before the site was assembled as it is today and then there was the development work to be funded. Everything had to be put into the effort. In went the pension plan, the big car and the mortgage-free status of the home. There was a nervous time when interest rates soared above 20%

It was an all-in play which was helped along immensely by one's in-house design skills (no £-million fee for a big name designer), by one's ability to operate heavy earth-shaping machinery (thus reducing contractor costs to a minimum), by one's simple approach which was to set-up golf for golf's sake without too many added trumpets and brass knobs, and by one's background in golf in the west of Ireland where one had observed how the game can be grown organically.

The 1990s heralded a new age in Irish golf as the game ceased being merely a game and became an industry and one which some newcomers seemed to feel was a bottomless pit of money as they splurged huge sums on clubhouses, fountains, flowerbeds and other peripherals. Even the old established members' co-operative clubs were infected by the spending fever and many of them began to market golf and thereby lose some of the tranquillity they always enjoyed.

This lemming-like rush into golf tourism by the co-operatives is quite amazing. Their core business is to provide good and peaceful golf for their members. But the whiff of business distracts some of them and they pay a big price in return for a share of the travelling golfer market.

As others threw cheque books and spreadsheets at their properties, sometimes getting too deeply in debt, we did a great deal of spending but kept the costs within our capacity to cover the situation by doing most of the work ourselves and by resolving to bring things along at our own financial pace, postponing elements like the clubhouse until they became necessary, rather than entering the instant grandeur stakes. After all, we only wanted to go golfing ourselves and welcome others to join in.

The ability to keep costs down created a situation whereby we never had to do marketing, we have never spent a cent on advertising other than for staff, and we didn't have to stand at the gate worrying whether paying guests would come to help pay the bills. With west of Ireland caution, never forgetting the observations of childhood, we stayed safely within our depth.

A BIG & BRAVE NAME

Claiming the golfing continent of Europe.

It is never easy agreeing on a name for a new child.   Books are consulted. Family trees and sensitivities are considered. Arguments and discussions ebb and flow. Eventually it gets done and very soon one wonders what all the fuss was about as the new member of the family becomes a part of the landscape.

Naming a golf course isn't much easier but complications were avoided as one played it close to one's chest and worked it out alone. Fun names were thought of. Like Pat's Pit and, maybe, Happy Hills. An early decision was not to name it after the local area as this often signifies ownership by the local community and that was not the case on this occasion.

Dozens of word combinations were written down, parsed, analysed and teased. Eventually the choice was made as three events provided valuable prompting.

One night, sitting exhausted in front of the television after a day of greenshaping one became awake to the fact that the old romantic classic films, always American made, invariably featured the heroes and heroines going on vacation to Europe. The name chosen would have to direct overseas golfers to us and a good start would be to get them onto the correct continent for openers. Europe would feature in the name.

At that time it became known that the European Union would come into existence in 1992 after the Treaty of Maastricht. We would be opening for play that year. So one had a second reason to consider the word Europe. Why not embrace our new identity as Europeans?

Finally, it all came together after a visit to The Country Club with my Boston journalist friend George Kimball. Drop-out "Country" and insert "European".   It could be The European Club!

The golfers get down to the seaside in earnest when play reaches the twelfth hole.

It looked good. It sounded good. It made a statement of intent. One day, this new links would be worthy of its name THE European Club. Everyday has been spent working in that direction.

Next came the choice of a logo. One wanted it to be Celtic. One wanted it to signify permanence and stability. It would have to have a golf image within.

As luck would have it we were building a golf course for the Quinn family at Ballymascanlon House in Dundalk at the time and their lands housed the Proleek Dolmen which we highlighted as the backdrop to a par-3 green. It was lovely.

Dolmens are to be found all over Ireland. They are the neolithic burial markers for important people, royalty in many cases, and they have stood for centuries. They feature three standing stones and a capping stone sitting on top. The stones frequently weigh over thirty tons and it remains a mystery how the people of old managed to build them without machinery.

A greater mystery surrounds the Proleek Dolmen. In building the golf course in adjoining fields we had reason to dig deep in places. But we never came upon another rock remotely as large as those used to make the dolmen, not even one-fiftieth the size, nothing bigger than a decent stone. The rocks in the dolmen must have been brought from afar. Legend has it that they were carried on-site by a Scottish giant named Parrah Boug MacShagean who is said to be buried nearby. Maybe the effort proved too much for him?

In any event, the dolmen was chosen as our logo and four huge rocks were imported from the Wicklow Mountains to create our very own one, perhaps the first dolmen to be built in centuries, along the pathway from the car-park to the clubhouse. Our overseas visitors really enjoy stopping at it and taking photographs as they are unlikely to see another one on their whirlwind golfing safari across the country.

A golf ball has been superimposed atop the dolmen for the print and statuette version of our logo and the whole effect is to proclaim Celtic durability for our golf enterprise. The plan is to produce miniatures of our dolmen in years ahead for use as paper-weights, bookends, table clocks, table lamps and other ornaments. These possibilities arise because of the three dimensional nature of the dolmen. We have patented the design just to be sure.

Great. We had a name and a logo and a golf links on the way. We decided to open for play on December 26, 1992 because at that time of year many of the inland courses in Ireland can be damp or closed by frost and the keenest players seek the linksland for their weekly fix.

The sixth hole is a tough par-3 with a stream running tight to the left of the green.

This had created problems around Dublin where there were a great many golfers and only a few links and it was impossible for those to accommodate the demand. We estimated that the golfers would come and they did.

Now, the golf links was quite raw at the time. We were following the traditional pattern of setting-up enough ground for golf and going about playing the game while developing onwards. So, a modest guest fee of £10 was offered and that proved so popular that there was a dawn traffic jam outside the gate on our first morning, and the next and the next and we have never closed for play since then.

We had no clubhouse to begin with but sat in a car taking those £10-notes in the window! Nobody complained. After a few weeks we rented some portable cabins and set-up changing and toilet facilities. We had a small coffee dock. It was homely and enjoyed by most.

The coffee was good. We always had good sandwiches and apple-tart and a welcome for those who came. All of the children, they were just kids at the time, contributed to the cause in the catering department with Sidon and Patrick, our twins, backing-up Gerard and Bernardine Jnr. and even little Zilla, the baby, trying her hand at drying dishes! This sense of family was just what one had hoped for as The European Club was planned as a central point for family life in the generations to come.

The Golfing Union of Ireland asked whether we would let their junior teams play training sessions over the links. We were delighted to oblige and totally thrilled when the young lads and the officials came in after their games and fairly devoured the roast beef and potatoes followed by plenty of apple-tart with cream and gallons of coffee prepared over the stove at home by Bernardine, my wife, and our children Sidon, Patrick and Zilla. The place was filled with laughter, the windows were steamed-up, and everyone enjoyed the very essence of golf.

Of course, in an age when golf was suddenly moving upmarket and golf courses were being dropped from heaven complete with gardens and fountains and palatial clubhouses, there had to be those who would not understand. Those who would not know how golf had got started through the ages and might view us as some kind of prehistoric creatures.

This set the scene for the day when four gentlemen arrived from a long established Dublin club and were clearly uncomfortable in our modest accommodations but too gentle to say anything. One could see that they had expected more and were not sure what to do next as they sipped their coffees.

The atmosphere thawed-out and our guests quickly relaxed when two large limousines arrived and two of our regular visitors of the time came golfing, but wanted to have a chat and some banter and coffee and apple-tart first, in the persons of the late Michael Wadsworth who was the Canadian Ambassador to Ireland (later to go to Notre Dame as director of athletics from 1995 to his untimely death in 2000) and Dr.Patrick Hillery the immediate past President of Ireland! What could be wrong with a situation that was clearly enjoyable to an ambassador and a president?

Dr. Hillery had started his golfing life at Spanish Point, not far from Lahinch where he was a member also, when life was simple and easy in that part of the world. He savoured the fine things in life but never lost the relaxed Irishness which allowed him to extract equal pleasure from simple things.

Ambassador Wadsworth was just a marvellously warm human who responded generously to friendship and made all around him feel his equal although he was a giant amongst men. His father, Bunny, starred for the Ottawa Rough Riders in 1940 and Michael became an all star Canadian Football League defensive lineman playing for De La Salle High School in Toronto and for the University of Notre Dame before a five year career with the Toronto Argonauts. He was on a winning Gruen Trophy team in 1966 and he was named an all star in 1968 after which he went into law, became an ambassador and ultimately returned to Notre Dame. We were sad when he left us and shocked when we heard of his death at the early age of 60. His likes does not pass the way often.

Another memorable event happened on the day that a group of very important New Yorkers arrived to play The European Club. Their chauffeur swept them in our gate, past our cabins, and up a dirt track into the links in search of the clubhouse. They were probably expecting to find a palace hidden in the hills in view of the name of the club! Instead, they got stuck in a sandpit and had to be pulled out by a tractor. When they returned to the cabins asking for directions to the palace they were astounded to be told --- YOU'RE IN THE CLUBHOUSE! To their credit, they adjusted quickly and had a good day's golf.

Domestically in Ireland we had little difficulty in having people understand what we were about at The European Club. Invitations were issued to some of the old clubs to send teams for a game and so we had matches with Royal County Down, Portmarnock, Ballybunion, Hermitage, Castle and Royal Dublin amongst others. They all enjoyed the thought that this was how their own great clubs had started life and it was gratifying to have confirmed one's theory that golfers are quite smart!

So it was that the peer pressures of the modern world didn't affect us at all as we set about establishing The European Club with the primary emphasis on the development of the golf links. If we succeeded, it was certain that all the ancillary facilities would fall into place in their own time.

HOMELESS GOLFERS

Learning how to organise golfers into a club.

There are always diversions along the way of life and so it happened in my inexorable journey towards the establishment of my own golf place and golf club. These diversions eat-up time but can often produce unexpected benefits as did my dalliance with a project called The Homeless Golfers.

This project was undertaken purely because of a young man's love for golf and golfers, one was aged about twenty-five and newly married and idealistic, but was to become a major task . The unexpected benefit was that it trained one in the organisation of golfers and helped prepare one for the structuring of The European Club many years later. It was a project, too, that one was uniquely equipped for and motivated to undertake.

When one moved to Dublin as a fledgling golf-writer in the mid-1960s, as the first person in Ireland to devote himself full-time to this profession, everyone was very kind both at the offices of the Evening Herald, for whom I eventually got to write five broadsheet pages of golf per week, and at the city golf clubs and those throughout the country.

Many of the clubs issued a card annually proclaiming one to be an honorary member. All of them made one welcome to play golf free of charge and pressed one to avail of free food and drink. What a wonderful position to find oneself in. They certainly knew how to treat a golf-writer back then!

Still, there was a flaw in the plot. A strong social conscience couldn't allow the fullest enjoyment of such luxuries without giving a thought to those thousands of people who could not get membership of a golf club, or gain a handicap, and so could never enjoy the game properly.

All of the clubs had full memberships and long waiting lists. Truly it could be seen that the word club gives a warm glow to those who belong but that it is a word signifying exclusion for those outside. It wasn't a good human situation and it wasn't good for golf.

There was a clear need for public golf courses at a time when nobody was really thinking of the private

This view of the sixth hole shows just how perilously close the stream is to some pin positions.

sector investor becoming involved. The Golfing Union of Ireland, with the late Dr. Gerry Owens as chief voice, was making noises about the need. But they weren't getting anywhere as the politicians didn't feel compelled by a need to help those in elite private clubs to propagate an elitist sport.

It was a time for action. Time to help Dublin gain a public golf course and help thousands of people into golf. It seemed a good idea to mobilise the city's golfers who did not have club memberships and demonstrate a social need for a public course. Why not form a group called The Homeless Golfers to create a non-elitist image for golf and gain political support?

It was with considerable confidence that one approached editor Aidan Pender, my mentor and great hero, with the idea which would also sell newspapers. Shock, horror, he said forget it.

Then he went on holidays and his brash young cub went ahead and wrote a column inviting those seeking club memberships to meet in the Waldorf-Astoria Hotel. Three people showed-up. Good, at least we had some life in the body so the next day's column announced that The Homeless Golfers' Association had been founded and inviting all and sundry to a further meeting the next week. Very quickly the numbers rose to hundreds and we were on our way. The next move was to get some golf for the Homeless Golfers so that the politicians could see them in action.

For political reasons and golfing reasons the golf had to be at an unsocial hour and really cheap. Now it was time for one to write an individual and very personal letter to every golf club in County Dublin asking whether they would grant a number of tee-times for an outing of Homeless Golfers ..... preferably shortly after dawn and at a greenfee of one shilling (about 5-cent)..... and every club responded quickly and positively! Angels all!

The three men who had attended the first meeting proved to be treasures as they got dug-in alongside one to organise things. The late Peter Dunne, a postal worker who was a member at Lucan Golf Club and need not have bothered, was indefatigable in the cause. Tony Hyland and Larry Courtney, both artisans at the Castle Golf Club, showed vision beyond their years and rallied to every call. One's brand new bride, Bernardine, not alone released one to spend all one's sparetime on the campaign but sat-up nights helping with a mountain of correspondence.

Our first golf outing was at Rush Golf Club. The second was at Elm Park Golf Club. The results were published in the press and it was made clear that these men had to get out of bed at dawn to get to the golf course and that each of them would have to sit-out many of the planned golf outings as our membership soared above one thousand people.

The second hole is a simply elegant par-3 with a well-bunkered green.

Those were great days and frustrating days. The golf clubs and the golfers were great. The politicians were devious and difficult to move. The late Noel Lemass, the government minister with responsibility for the Phoenix Park, was an exception as he listened to the pleas for a course there and even attended our meetings and an annual dinner. There was a precedent for golf in the park as The Royal Dublin Golf Club had been founded there before moving out to the linksland at Dollymount.

It was a difficult political call as golf's elitist image didn't help and there were many people clearly out to defend the open aspect of the great park for the entire population. Hope sprang-up when further lands beyond the River Liffey were acquired for an extension to the Phoenix Park. Surely a nine-hole course could be established there?

Lemass was interested and even employed the late Eddie Hackett to draw-up a route plan for a possible course. No good. Someone else produced a plan to build a new road through the site and won the day. An election saw Lemass removed from office and that moment had passed.

Then there came a new ray of hope when the Corballis Golf Club vacated its lovely links in north-Dublin to transform itself into Forrest Little Golf Club near Dublin Airport. Their old links became the property of Dublin County Council. Great! But no! They were going to discontinue the golf links and establish a public park in its place. Enough!

It would be one thing if the politicians failed to establish a new golf course but it would be totally unthinkable that they should close down a perfectly good golf course that the county now owned.

They were a distressing bunch to deal with. Several times we stood outside the meeting rooms to see what they decided about the golf project. Brazenly they would emerge to say that they had tried to promote the cause, virtually every one of them, but somehow it had been defeated.

The relentless pressure told in the end, however, and eventually came the announcement that Dublin was to have its very own public golf course! Shamelessly, the politicians who had campaigned most against the cause went around seeking to take credit for it! One wasn't invited to the opening.

No matter. There was still work to be done as playing golf on a public course solved only half of the problem. If the golfers could earn handicaps they could play at the public course and also seek entry to the open competitions run by clubs all over the country and so enjoy the game more fully.

Three difficulties arose: (a) The Golfing Union of Ireland would not allow anybody other than an affiliated club administer handicaps; (b) The Golfing Union of Ireland would not affiliate a club that did not have a right to play golf on an established golf course and have a clubhoue of its own; and (c)

Dublin County Council would not allow golfers on the public course to form a club. It looked like a totally impossible situation.

We were not for turning, however, and declared that The Homeless Golfers Association had been disbanded and had been transformed into the Dublin & County Golf Club playing its golf at Corballis. Nobody could stop our players booking games just like any other citizen.

Fate continued to deal good cards as one became aware that a small holiday home right beside the first tee of the public course, and not separated from it by fencing of any kind, could be bought from the widow of Brendan Herlihy who had won the Irish Amateur Close Championship in 1950 and had kept his game sweet here. The Herlihy family proved most receptive to the idea and a price was agreed.

Money was scarce, of course, and once more minor miracles were needed. This one took the shape of my vibrant friendship with the late Jack Cantwell who was president of Tramore Golf Club as I responded to his calls for publicity for that club and the great scratch cup tournament it played annually. One of his sons was a bank manager in Dublin and he agreed to advance the money on my young signature and we had a clubhouse!

It was now a formality that the Golfing Union of Ireland would affiliate the club and allow members to earn handicaps.

Ironically, one's departure from the club was not bitter but it was less than sweet. Dublin County Council erected a fence between our clubhouse and the golf course. I had it removed as it was clear that they were seeking to eliminate a well established right-of-way. They repaired it. I had it removed again. They repaired it again and a meeting of the club council instructed me to leave it at that.

That was the final meeting of the club that one attended as one decided to go off, having done all that one could to get more players into the game, to play one's own golf and concentrate on one's family and professional obligations. The move was taken in the knowledge that the club would get on fine, as clubs do when officials change, and so it has as it moved over the road to a course of its very own under the name of Balcarrick Golf Club and soon it boasted a fine facility and over 800 members.

Those were exciting times and it turned-out that Dublin County Council did one a favour by putting-up that fence. It provoked my release from an arduous commitment to the cause of other people's golf and released me to pursue the dream of a golf place of my own.

All the politics, all the financial worries, all the nights of envelope filling, all the arguments about competition rules and handicaps had trained one quite unwittingly for what was to follow.

NASTY OPPOSITION

The shock of being a hate figure

There were some shocks to the system as one set about establishing a golf links at Brittas Bay. One hadn't imagined that anyone would object to a project which would transform a wilderness into a thing of beauty, bring joy to thousands of people each year as they got to take healthy exercise in a lovely place, and give good employment.

Much less was one prepared for the sheer deviousness, venom and hatred to be encountered in the early days.

The first unpleasant experience arose when a registered letter arrived from Wicklow County Council ordering that the work be stopped. It stated that we were in breach of planning law in a number of respects and cited reasons which one instantly recognised to be wrong. One had been involved in golf course design for years and knew that golf course development was exempt from planning at that time subject to a number of very clear and very simple conditions. The best legal advice had been taken specific to our lands before the start.

So a letter was sent to the Council stating our case and that we were going to proceed with the work. Just as well, too, because it wasn't long until the planning laws changed and we would have been halted under the new legislation if we had hesitated. This happened in at least one other case in another county, where a golf links was ensnared in delays until the new laws came in to halt it, and one has never come to terms with the way in which some public bodies can be so devious. It is sad when honesty, transparency and fair dealing cannot be expected from public bodies.

The same can be said of some of the professional classes and especially of those who use the gravitas associated with professorships and doctorates in the public mind to promote their own distorted and

40

The fifth hole invites a running approach and is dedicated to a master of the craft, Peter Thomson.

often underdeveloped view of the planet. One medical man penned a letter expressing the wish that one would burn in hell for introducing golf to the dunes!

Others weren't as brave and settled for shooting from the bushes. Having purloined the word environmentalist to describe themselves, thus effectively putting everyone who disagrees with them into the category of anti-environmentalist, they set about writing to government and to the European powers in Brussels asking that the project be stopped and the grant withdrawn. They wrote inaccurate accusations and downright lies to the press and, of course, on the internet which is the home of free speech and ramblings for the weird and wonderful.

A common denominator for many of these people is cowardice and, at very least, an amazing lack of consideration for the lives of those fellow humans they choose to attack. Not one of these enemies had the style or the courage to write to one, to call and talk to one or to seek a meeting and a discussion. Their style is to campaign surreptitiously from the universities, with addresses therein giving an aura of intellectualism to what can be unbalanced ravings, and from the corridors of bureaucratic power.

Of course, there are good environmentalists out there. There are serious environmental issues to be addressed. But golf is not the world's big problem and it can, in fact, answer in part the need to give man a great recreational outlet in a way that does not upset the greater plan of things.

Happily, the majority of environmentalists are right-minded and considerate people with a wish to see the planet prosper with all who live on it. Nobody in their right mind, including golfers, can have a problem with that. But it is very difficult to endure the sneaky cantaloupes, those who are green on the outside but red on the inside, who use the environment as a weapon to advance extreme socialist thinking.

Happily, these matters have not been a cause of particular concern to The European Club for many years past and the golf links has been recognised as a very good one internationally and even a few of those who objected to its development have been seen to enjoy a game or two. It has taken a degree of self-control not to accord them a special welcome!

Meantime, decades of happy involvement in all aspects of the game prepared one for the big task of creating The European Club and developing its philosophy of simple enjoyment of an elementary game. Earliest memories include golf. Memories from the 1950s which was a pivotal time between old golf and new golf.   A time when some of the smaller rural clubs in Ireland still cut some grass by horse-drawn mower. A time when only the older and more posh clubs had elaborate clubhouses or any clubhouse. When money was scarce and Europe was just recovering from war. They were good times. The only down times were spent in the back row in school, looking out the window at perfect golfing weather, doodling images of golf holes in every white space available in every textbook. Every hole that one had played from Rosses Point through Ballymote, Ballina and Boyle to one's first visit to the great Portmarnock was sketched and analysed not from an architectural viewpoint but from the playing aspect. How could one have done better and how could one score lower next time out?

An interest in the workings of a golf course emerged. Watching the greenkeepers at Rosses Point trying to keep the greens alive in Summer, walking around splashing water bucket by bucket, caused a young mind to devise a plan for placing concrete saucers under greens so that water would be trapped in the root zone. That was one kid's solution to drought at a time when piped irrigation was still in the future and even Jack Nicklaus had yet to come along.

Another set of drawings was inspired by the frustration of watching the early television coverage of the game. Too many cameras and too many people were needed to make a telecast with cumbersome equipment and coverage was invariably confined to just a few holes.

It seemed obvious to a young mind that tournament golf courses should be arranged more like football fields with partially parallel holes running up and down towards embankments at either end. Those embankments could give thousands of spectators a perfect view and a narrow gauge railway on top of each could shuttle television cameras along and allow economic and timely coverage of every hole!

Sketches were prepared and sent to the PGA in America, to the R&A in Scotland, to the American television stations and to the BBC. Letters went to tournament sponsors whose events stood to gain enormously if television did a better job. But all went unanswered and fame and fortune eluded one. Looking back, though it was not evident at the time, it can be seen that the genesis had emerged of a career in golf writing, golf course design and golf course ownership.

Books from the local library played a big part in those formative days. One read about the great champions and how to play the game properly. There were stories of the old clubs in Scotland using local inns for their clubhouses in their early days and how the Royal County Down Golf Club used a waiting room at the local railway station as club headquarters for years until they were ready to build an actual clubhouse. Augusta was gaining notoriety as a beautiful place having ceased the grazing of cattle and turkeys on the course to stave-off bankruptcy after the war!

Those were simpler times and they ingrained in the mind that a golf course and club can be grown organically, as an evolutionary process, over several years. A valuable observation to have on-board when setting-up a club of one's own decades later when it would have been so attractive but possibly financially disastrous to try to run before one could walk.

Similarly, one learned the basics of golf course design at the coal face. Most golf clubs were based on rented farmland in those days and there was always tension between landlord and tenant as the farmer would wish to save some grass for cattle fodder and the golfers would want to cut more grass in order to find their golf balls. Evictions were frequent as happened in Ballymote, the small town in which one spent many happy childhood days, no fewer than three times while one was a teenager.

Three times, one sat on the back of a truck as dad and his friends went around town borrowing lawnmowers, not a common possession in those days, and then headed out the country to the site of our new golf course. It would take a week for those volunteers to mow-out square areas, rounded greens were a thing of the future, for nine greens and fence them with barbed wire to keep cattle and sheep off. Then, the flags would be popped-in, markers placed for the tees and the club was back in business and would improve matters as time went by.

Those greens were slow and bumpy. The fences were in the way and one got to drop another ball and play the shot again if an approach shot or a chip shot hit the wire. But it was a golf amongst friends and we loved it. It didn't seem weird or depressing. It was exciting and great fun at a time when memories still abounded of golf course grasses being cut by a scythe. Even at St. Andrews they mowed their greens by hand-scythe until long after the first lawnmower was patented in 1830 by a fellow who adapted to grass-cutting the machinery he had seen trimming rough wool carpets in the mills at Stroud in England. Ransomes became the first to secure a licence to produce these magical new machines, which have effectively made modern golf a possibility, and the first American licence for lawnmower production was taken-up as late as 1868.

Life was simple off-course as well. Only two golf clubs in Connacht, the County Sligo and Galway clubs, had stone-built clubhouses. The others all operated in tiny tin huts and only a few had a bar. Boyle Golf Club was a terrific place as Tommy Conroy was at once the best golfer in the district, the landowner and a skilled drummer. The parties in the tiny tin clubhouse were lively and wiped away any bad memories of poor golf played on a tiny course shared with sheep, ducks and geese ... nobody licked a golf ball there!

Childhood memories abound of going around and around the tiny putting green in the beams of light coming from the windows of that tiny clubhouse. Once in a while a window would open and a fatherly hand would place a glass of lemonade and a packet of crisps on the sill for his son, caddy and playing partner. What a life!

A few miles away in Ballaghaderreen life was even more simple. The course was more manicured but the clubhouse was a one-roomed tin shack, with no toilet facilities, measuring about 10-feet by 10-feet. Players hung their coats on nails in the wall and the Bishop of Achonry hung his on the next nail and everyone went golfing.

Greenfees, as at most clubs, were paid on the honesty box system, as there were no club employees to supervise matters, whereby the shilling or other fee was slipped into an envelope on which one wrote one's name before slipping it into the box.

Those were unhurried days when it was quite common to arrive at a golf course and find oneself all alone. There would be no staff, no other golfers, and no prospect of anyone coming along soon.

It could be lonely out there and quite frightening for a townsman until he developed a oneness with the landscape. Which possibly explains why golfers learned to move in cannibal packs seeking to feed off the golfing weaknesses of their friends. To be a winner one must find a loser!

Friends who had developed a thirst on the Ballaghaderreen course would stop-off at Sailor McDonagh's pub on the way home and relive the day and settle bets while sitting on a bag of flour or a side of bacon. Golf was the thing, pure and simple, played for its own sake and not taken as a walk between pints, as a social or business ladder or as a profit centre.

When a family membership was acquired at the County Sligo Golf Club at Rosses Point the game became more sophisticated. Clean-shoe golf all year through and no fences around the greens or animals on the course. Even so, it was still a joy to go golfing anywhere and one learned that the game is glorious no matter where it is played. Unwittingly, all of this served to sow the seeds of golf course design and golf club organisation in a young mind.

One was in at the grass-roots and got to see and understand the very simple essence of the game which can be summarised:- man, club, ball, grass short enough to find the ball, time to play and someone to beat! Bigger and better courses, bigger and better clubhouses, and better fairways and greens were just extensions of the basics and could be achieved through high finance or through patience. One chose to be patient.

DESIGNING THE DREAM

We are on the move at last

The modern style is to build a golf course very quickly and open it for play within two years of turning the first sod.   This is made necessary by the high finance approach with millions on the line upfront through site purchase, professional planning fees, contractor fees and, more often than not nowadays, the rapid sale of housing units and hotel bedrooms depending on quick and stylish delivery.

The majority of golf developments nowadays are simple and direct commercial undertakings with the accountants calling the shots whenever the going gets tight.   One fears that all too often the golf designs are compromised.

The European Club does not relate to this template.   The original motivation, way back in the 1950s, was golf for golf's sake. Pure and simple. Nothing has changed.

The plan was to have a golf course of one's own and to enjoy it.   Nothing has changed.

It was hoped that the golf course would be good enough to attract one's golfing friends for a game and that they would enjoy it. Nothing has changed, except that The European Club is bigger and better than one could have dared dream of in the 1950s, the 1960s or the 1970s and it is attracting new golfing friends from around the world.

Golf courses fall into two broad categories. Those built by locals for local people and which attract little outside interest; and those which get to welcome a steady parade of the curious and the great as they come to play.   This lesson was highlighted at Lahinch one wet day back in about 1972.

It had been raining all morning. Brud Slattery, the legendary local champion and club secretary, and I had talked ourselves to a frazzle so I went and sat out in the porch along with the club's goats to get out of his way.

After a time the goats, who acted as weather forecasters by coming into the clubhouse porch when bad

The green at hole 7a, one of our two extra holes, is one of my favourite places on the links.

weather was nearby, lived up to their reputations by moving out onto the links some minutes before the skies cleared and it was golftime once more!

Just then a slightly built figure dressed in conservative brown came across the car-park with a Sunday bag slung on shoulder. Could we play a few holes together?, he asked. Away we went into a great adventure as it turned out, it took to about The Dell to get to know each other's backgrounds, that he was none other than Jack Westland who lost to Francis Ouimet in the final of the 1931 U.S. Amateur Championship and came back in 1952 at age 46 to become the oldest ever winner of that title when overcoming Al Mengert in the final!

What an unassuming man. He had played Walker Cup and captained America in that event, he had served twelve years in the House of Representatives, was now residing at Cypress Point and was happy to play a few holes with anyone! We became good friends to his death in 1981 and all that one could hope for was that golf would continue to be that sort of game which unites people of different backgrounds and achievements.

So it was that work commenced on creating the links at The European Club with a mind crammed with images, memories and plans. How to proceed was a big question. All one's design work to date had been inland and one had never built a links before. The questions were legion ranging from the infertility of sand to the problems relating to the stabilisation of any sand to be exposed during construction. Legends abounded of sand moving so fast in storms of old that entire villages had been buried overnight. It was all a bit scarey.

The first move was to visit Ballybunion and talk to club manager Sean Walsh about their experiences in building their new links. As always, he was most hospitable and told me all he knew including stories of spreading animal slurry to stabilise and enrich the new fairways. Most helpful of all, he showed me pictures of work in progress with huge areas of sand exposed. All it lacked was camels and Lawrence of Arabia! The future looked daunting.

It was best to get moving and that is what we did. Luckily, soon after work got underway we had a most welcome visit from Paddy Caul who had played golf for Ireland and, most importantly, was head greenkeeper at The Island Golf Club where they had just implemented substantial extensions and improvements. He was appalled at the amount of sand which we had exposed at one time, maybe five or six fairways, and he lectured one roundly to the effect that everything would blow away if we hit a dry spell with wind. He described in graphic detail some of the horrors which had befallen them. We

48

The second of our two extra holes, it is called 12a, is a magnificent beast of a par-3.

hastened to secure that which we had disturbed before going further and just as well, too, as we were about to enter the pits of hell getting grass to grow. Several times greens were shaped and sown only to find that they had blown away, sometimes to a depth of four or five feet, within a few days. It was mildly surprising that ships going by on the Irish Sea didn't have to fit grass-cutters to mow their way through that part of their voyages .... our grass had to be out there somewhere!

Lessons were learned fast and very soon we started to install wind-breaking fences around each portion of ground as it was seeded and to keep it wet. That had its drawbacks initially as the bottoms of the fence materials which were in contact with the ground flapped and created nine or ten inch wide naked lines through the developing sward. The solution was to leave a gap of a few inches between the bottom of the fence material and the ground and eliminate contact in that way.

Those were difficult days and there is no point in seeking to romanticise them. Wife and children frequently joined part-time a growing band of permanent workers. At peak we had about thirty men hand-stitching marram grass in the dunes, watering troublesome areas, and performing by hand all the tasks which one didn't wish to use heavy machinery on. It took concentrated effort for a golf-writer to fund all of this and fridays could have been massacre days if one failed to produce!

The family album has pictures of Bernardine and Gerard, devoted wife and oldest son, on their hands and knees weeding the eleventh green one Sunday morning. Bernardine Jnr, who went on to be our chief fairway mower, joined the fray; the twins Sidon and Patrick have been magnificent at the front of the house for years working all hours as required; and Zilla answers all emergencies. Nobody could fail with a small and unwaveringly loyal army like that in support.

It was gratifying to see them all play their part and one can never forget the images of Gerard, at age thirteen or fourteen, learning to operate a big excavator and drive a big dump-truck. Not too many kids can have been so involved in the development of golf holes. Not since one had been out with dad and his friends reorganising a place to play in Ballymote!

As far as the family was concerned it was a real pioneering situation, operating along the lines that had been seen in family businesses and at smaller golf clubs in the west of Ireland a few years earlier, and we were bemused and sometimes amused by the reaction of observers who often misinterpreted it all as a place in trouble or going nowhere. We were going places and we knew it; and far from being in trouble we were one of the most financially sound golf developments in the country as costs were spread over a number of years rather than being covered with lump sum borrowings.

50

By going along steadily the finances didn't overheat and were helped by incomes from concurrent design work at St. Margaret's, Druid's Glen, Connemara Isles, Wicklow and Ballymascanlon.

One man stood out as a giant at this time. Gerry Arthur joined the staff in its earliest days and was soon recognised as a special person. He didn't know anything about golf but he wanted to work and he was left alone for days on end, while one went away to other jobs, moving sand and keeping grass growing as directed. He never failed then nor has he ever failed to this day when he is our trusted head greenkeeper and friend. He leads a dedicated team with Richard Lambert, Pat Dickenson, Joey Kavanagh and Larry Brennan all having been on-board from very early days.

Another gain from the slow but sure process was that one had plenty of time in which to think-out design elements and work upon them in detail. Here alone there is none of the frustration of being unable to improve one's design because the owner is happy to leave things as they are. Here alone the golfing muses can be entertained year after year.

Design is, of course, central to the success of a golf course and that is why one actually enjoyed the fact that work was progressing steadily rather than rapidly. There was time to think and one is still thinking twenty years later and proposes to continue this process while energy allows. The game is evolving too fast to rest on one's laurels and, besides, every year one's own knowledge of the game and design moves along and has to be taken into account. This gives the best chance of landing-up with a classic or, at least, the very best that the land and one's imagination and brain can yield.

The initial route plan has stood the test of time. It is a marvellous route in many ways. It affords sea views from all or part of fifteen holes as well as from the two extra holes which have been added over the years. It brings the player into dales, through high dunes, along a glorious marsh and to the very edge of the beach on a march which is intended to challenge the fibre of the golfing soul while divorcing the golfer from the pressures of the world outside. Each hole is designed as a fifteen-minute sanctuary, a portion of the golfer's life which must be spent with care, where a player can submerge in self.

At The European Club there is no distracting housing, no adjoining highway, no noise from low flying planes such as are found at so many otherwise classic courses today, no trains racing by and no beverage carts. Many people are amazed to find that there is no radio or television in the clubhouse. This is a place for golf and for conversation!

It is a place also for design and redesign as one strives to make something that is good even better.

KEEPING PACE WITH TECHNOLOGY

The links gets longer and gains more bunkers

The original plan was to create The European Club as a golfing place for oneself. That has not been lost sight of.   It has just got bigger around the original concept. But with a very small membership, which has never been allowed to rise above one hundred and fifty people, it is possible to take the place very, very private anyday by confining golf to members only and that means that ten or fewer players will appear on a weekday rising to about thirty on a busy Sunday. Places don't come much more private than that.

The links is closed completely for a few days at Christmas each year and is closed to all but members whenever a private party, such as one's birthday, is to be celebrated. What an enjoyable indulgence. The same can be said for the long hours most days when the links is quite deserted and one can relive the good old days of the 1950s at Rosses Point or Ballymote by emptying a bag of balls onto a fairway or into a bunker and playing them without stress or fuss.

Of course, part of the fun is sharing the joys of life with others and so we welcome guests most days of the year on the basis of a guest fee, a small contribution to the upkeep of the place, and on the understanding that we try to play the game quietly, uncrowded as possible and with consideration for others. Part of the problem with this is that many people are so introverted that they do not seem to realise that their ultra-slow or ultra-fast play is a grave irritant to those behind them or in front of them. It can be tiresome trying to keep everyone happy.

The ninth hole bends left around a stand of gorse, gorgeous when in bloom, to a green with a half-open front door.

It is tiresome, too, having to clean-up after those modern players who take the liberty of not raking bunkers, not replacing divots and not repairing pitch marks. The advice to staff is to try to be blind to offenders, try to be deaf and be slow to speech. But it is our policy to ask the worst offenders to leave the links, only after being cautioned more than once and failing to adjust their behaviour, but that is a relatively rare occurrence and one which is very upsetting for everyone concerned. Not to take a stance, however, is to invite chaos.

The original plan came under stress in another most unexpected way. The game has changed utterly in the space of two decades. The distance the ball can be made travel is the biggest single change although the lob wedge and the belly-putter have helped the dramatic transformation along. As we seek to keep our links in the upper ranks of fine golf courses we have to take cognisance of all this and change the layout suitably.

Many of these changes hardly impact the average player, who has a choice of tees from which to play, but are designed to maintain a challenge for the best players. So it is an irritant when players who over-estimate their powers seek to play off the back-tees and then go away to tell the world that The European Club is unreasonably long and tough. They shouldn't call it murder but suicide when they choose tees unwisely in that way.

Back in 1993, our first year in operation, John Daly was the longest hitter in tournament golf with an average drive of 288.9-yards. By 2003, there were fifty-six players averaging longer than that and the 350-yard drive had come to stay. In the first half of 2007 no fewer than one hundred players on the American and European Tours were beating Daly's old mark as a matter of routine.

Quite suddenly we were playing a different game. It had got to where the best players hardly ever found a need to use the longest clubs. The new drivers and golf balls removed the brassey, the spoon (except for some tee work), the one-iron and the two-iron from the bag. How often does one see the today's champion clip a driver off the fairway in order to gain advantage over his less talented foe?

It all became quite ridiculous at the (British) Open Championship at Muirfield in 2002. Nobody has written about it. There seems to be a reluctance to pass comment on strange events at great places but this was not always so as the legendary Andrew Kirkaldy once referred to the links at Muirfield, which suffered from dampness in the early days, as "an auld water-meddy".

It had a meadowish look again in 2002 with the rough grown deliberately elbow-high and they had to place two or three forecaddies on each side of each hole to avoid the embarrassment of a factory-full of golf balls being lost. As a result, everyone played irons off most tees and then hit medium or short irons to the greens on even the longest par-4s. Without wind they were in a strange place.

It may be that the days are gone when only the best brains in golf have a game plan and the rest just founder. But it is sad if there is only one possible game plan as at Muirfield in 2002 and, even at that, there was a crucial lost ball incident as Gary Evans missed the seventy-first green and missed the playoff by one stroke when the ball was lost despite the presence of forecaddies, caddies, players, officials and spectators.

Strangely enough, the very next Open Championship was to feature another remarkable lost ball incident as Tiger Woods hooked his opening drive into oblivion at Royal St. George's.

These lost balls were a result of both the R&A and the USGA using rough grass as one of their major weapons to challenge the modern golfer and it is difficult to see how this can be changed unless they do something to curb the equipment manufacturers.

Against this background one decided that our links should grow from an initial championship measurement of 6,729-yards in 1993 to a level of 7,355-yards in 2006. Hopefully, things will settle down soon or most golf courses on the planet will have to buy more land or become no more than pitch-and-putt for the top professional and amateur players and outright dangerous for everyone else as unskilled players scatter balls further and further afield.

It is amazing how the R&A and the USGA have allowed this dog to run so far with just a few manufacturers making hefty profits while all the golf courses have had to spend billions to keep pace. The tail is wagging the dog for sure.

Happily, we are in position to follow the ball all the way up to 8,500-yards without buying land but sincerely hope it doesn't come to that as it is doubtful whether most golfers will be able to walk that far, or be able to afford the time to do so, and golf carts will need to have turbos fitted!

These thoughts are a bit amusing when presented in a certain way. But the debate is deadly serious as, apart from extending existing courses to keep them valid, more and more sites that would have been ideal for a new golf course twenty years ago are now too small for the purpose. So, the smart men at the equipment companies are limiting the future of the game.

How the powers-that-be allow this to go on is a mystery. It could not happen in football, imagine all the stadia having to be enlarged!, or in tennis or in basketball. It should not be allowed in golf.

A neat answer to it all would be if the amateur golfers stopped buying the golf balls manufactured by the companies that are causing golf courses to become obsolete to the great cost of those amateurs. It would be as simple as clubs deciding to nominate different brands for use in club events just as has been discussed in relation to Augusta and The Masters. Tennis clubs have followed this line for years and even enjoy sponsorships to ensure that a given ball is the chosen one. An unlikely scenario in golf but a serious proposition if things continue to get worse.

It was around 2000 that one took the unimaginable step of stretching one of our par-4s to 460-yards, two to 470-yards and one to 477-yards. It was a little worrying to go so far into uncharted waters. It could have been the subject of savage criticism if misunderstood. One needn't have worried as such huge par-4s soon became well known in tournament play and some people went so far as to introduce the 500-yard par-4. Soon after that it came as a shock to have one magazine writer describe our seventeenth, newly extended to 432-yards, as a short par-4! Wow!

It seems inevitable that our lovely 499-yard par-3 third hole will become a par-4 for tournament play at some future date and that will bring our overall par down to seventy.

Today, none of our par-4s measures less than 400-yards off the championship tees but seven of the thirteen do so off the regular members' tees; and only two of the par-4s measures over 400-yards off the forward members' tees. That looks like a nice balanced presentation and it gives all sorts of game options to all sorts of players.

When it comes to par-3s we are truly blessed with a choice of five from which to have three in play. In other words, we have introduced two extra par-3s and invite our golfers to play all twenty holes at all but the busiest times. They love it.

The original layout has the par-3s falling at holes two, six and fourteen. These are nicely varied as they point in different directions to maximise the wind factor and can be played at anything up to 160, 210 and 195-yards respectively. The two newcomers are lovely additions and as different as siblings can be. Hole 7a is 160-yards off the tips but is normally played as a tricky 120-yards to a green which is tilted quite savagely and offers either a handy birdie or an opportunity to reach for the blood pressure pills as three putts loom. Hole 12a is a different matter as it is, if you wish, a big brother reverse image of Calamity Corner at Portrush with a green sitting on a lovely platform high in the dunes and playing anything from 160 to 205-yards for the boys. This golf hole is a cracker!

People ask why do we have two extra holes? The quick answer to that is - Why not? The first of two longer answers is that two beautiful greensites sat out there begging to be used. They could not be

The tenth green is approached through a narrow passage between two dunes. It widens at the green.

fitted into a route for 18-holes so why not go to 20-holes? The second long answer is that those who like to play golf like to play lots of it so why stop at 18-holes? If you are going out to play golf play plenty of it because family and business ties may keep you off the links for days or weeks to come. The two extra holes bring many practical benefits.

For example, when we are working maintenance or design changes on a hole or two we can take them out of play and still have 18-holes in play.

They come in very handy on busy days when play tends to slow down. We can let the first two-thirds of the field play just the original 18-holes and have the late starters play all 20-holes as they find playing extra holes preferable to standing about on tee-boxes at the back of a slow moving field.

Another benefit of the two extra holes is that they bring the links up to two loops of ten holes, very appropriate as metric goes well with things European, and this gives us extra time to get games started on those days that we are using a two-tee start! A fun outcome is that we have holes with handicap indexes of nineteen and twenty and this goes down well with lower handicapped players as they have fewer holes on which to concede two strokes. That provokes a lot of debate.

Design is much more complex than yardages and so one has devoted a lot of time to the placement and shaping of hazards over the years. All of our bunkers, for example, were perfectly placed to be a factor for all classes of players on opening day. One was pleased that this had been done using only sixty-nine bunkers as one wished to stay towards the Augusta subdued approach in this regard, even though we don't have water in play at five holes as they do or their trees and sharply sloping and glazed greens, than the scatter cushion approach at Lytham.

Then the game changed and our links changed. The ramifications of championship tees further back had to be considered. Also the fact that players were now approaching greens with less club meant that thought had to be given to the tightness of bunkering around the greens. It was a puzzler.

The first instinct was to move some of the existing bunkers but this didn't give a complete answer everytime as it opened-up the defences by leaving open spaces just as when football defenders are drawn from their positions. This would happen in particular if a fairway bunker was moved further away from a tee. Good, but it left now unguarded space for the players to blaze away at and get closer to the green unimpeded.

The only solution was to introduce more bunkers. Eighteen extra in all to bring our total stock to ninety-seven. This is still on the low side of the average number of bunkers on a major golf course and we are happy with that because ours are, for the moment at least, just where they are needed.

Some of the newcomers, particularly those on holes four, nine and eighteen serve not alone as hazards but as significant definers for the tee-shots on dog-leg holes. Look at our links guide, glance at the bunkers and the game is on. Pick your bunker to aim at or to try to slide the ball past and play on.

In the process one conceived the idea of lining all of the bunkers with railway sleepers. This is an old Scottish idea born in the days when the railway companies threw unwanted sleepers over the fence onto the adjoining golf links at places like Prestwick and where they were snapped-up by the pioneering greenkeepers and used to shore-up tees, embankments and bunker faces. One always liked the look of them.

Not everyone likes the timber, of course, and one man who disliked the sleepers is Ryder Cup player Eamonn Darcy who said so quite openly until his ball rebounded off one for a hole-in-one at the second one day. That is one way to gain a convert.

Sleepers give great visual definition to our links and answer two problems. First of all they allow us to show players where the bunkers are by having them pop their brown heads out of the green landscape. This is a big improvement on the hidden bunkers which generally afflict links golf as they have to be dug deep into the ground to prevent the winds from whipping all the sand away. The sleepers provide perfect aerodynamics and smooth surfaces to allow the blown sands to whirl about and fall back into the pit.

Sleepers have another virtue in that they are much more durable than revetted sod faces, which need replacement every five or six years, while allowing us to get the bunkers close into the greens in the same way as the revetting does.

It looks like the sleepered bunkers are here to stay for a long time. Meantime, it is fun thinking that our bunkers are the only ones in the world which could be burned to the ground!

All of this was worked-out over a number of years and one is very happy with the situation as it stands today. Adding to the happiness is the clear knowledge that one can redesign any element of the golf course one wishes at anytime without going to a committee or owner for permission.

So much has happened since opening day, and continues to happen, that one sees it as a clear advantage to move slowly on design. It is a true blessing to have the freedom to do so without having any feature so revered that it is not subject to consideration for review. Once a golf course is monumentalised it begins to die in design terms.

OPTICAL ILLUSIONS

Training in photography pays design dividends

The fact that one has carried a camera everywhere one has gone in golf since about 1960 and taken pictures at tournaments and of golf courses through all those years contributed a great deal to the design of the links of The European Club.

We live in an age when the golfers like to play by numbers. They want to know the distances to the hazards and to the flags. They have more information than any previous generation of players.

They have better equipment than ever before and they are well fed. Yet, most of them don't play the game any better than before and legions of poor players can be seen marching about with arsenals of the very best equipment but failing to score too good.

Sadly for them, and happily for the golf course designer, they are just as poor sighted and nervous as their predecessors and so are open to doubt. They have all been wired with faulty nervous systems and so they are prone to confusion.

Indeed, many of them are so confused and deluded that they leave their families and businesses for prolonged periods in search of something on the fairways. It cannot be the walk alone. Or the scenery. Or the company. It is something more primeval than that and related to the hunting instinct which has been embedded in mankind over millennia. Men who hunt golf balls are interesting studies and this is where the fun interface between the golf course (the hunted) and the hunter lies.

Optical illusions and a wee touch of intimidation form a part of the defence system of any good golf course and, to a huge degree, these two elements walk hand-in-hand because an awareness that illusions exist creates destructive doubt in the mind of the hunter.

Photography is all about optics, of course, and the creation and the distortion of proportions and images. Different perspectives, different framing and different lenses can alter almost beyond recognition the perception of a given landscape such as a golf hole.

60

The sixteenth has been transformed into a lovely hole since the bunker on the right replaced an old farm fence.

Lessons learned from a study of depth of field provide a clear example of one type of illusion. Place a person to be photographed in a way that there is a background building or wall some distance behind them and use a slightly longer lens and the picture will condense the distance between the subject person and the background object to the point that they seem to be joined together. Even hundreds of yards can be lost visually in this way.

Look around you anywhere. Focus on an object that stands on its own, a parked motor car for instance, keeping it between you and a slightly distant wall and notice how the yardage between the car and the wall does not seem to exist anymore. This illusion can be transferred into the golfing landscape in many ways and wreak havoc with the confidence of the golfer trying to assess a shot.

One application of this craft on a golf course is to place a green in such a way that there is a backing hill or line of trees. The green becomes visually condensed to the point that it looks tiny and the relative visual bulk of the background makes the distance to be traversed by the golf ball look shorter than it is.

Remove that background object and the shot looks longer and the green looks bigger. Place framing hills or trees to either side of the fairway in the approach and you are suddenly looking through the wrong end of a telescope as the shot is now visually very long.

Hidden dips, concealing yards and yards of ground to be travelled over, create doubt in the mind of the player armed with the yardages. Surely, his eyes tell him, these yardages are wrong!

A related skill one employs is to have hillocks protruding along the edges of fairways and shielding or partially shielding substantial areas of fairway from view. In this way even generous target areas can be made to look miserably and dangerously small. Standing on the seventh tee at The European Club yields a dramatic version of this set-up as the target looks like a ribbon whereas it is really ninety yards wide where drives are expected to land.

The presence of mountain backdrops or of ocean waves is of great assistance to the golf course designer as the orientation of roll and fall is distorted. Just stand on the beach and look at the sea. It looks as though it is running away uphill to the horizon! If you think that what you see is true you had better start running because that water is going to flow right in on top of you!

Greens placed close to such confusing images can be made a nightmare for the golfer as the clever designer can juxtapose the shapes he is building in such a manner as to make the putts virtually impossible to read. The most drastic samples of this will, for example, convince the golfer that the putt is uphill when viewed from behind the ball but downhill when viewed from behind the hole.

Golf course design is at its most sadistic when it distorts the actual distances involved in carries from the tee and carries across rough or other hazards to the green. Players can be encouraged to hit too hard or too soft and to overshoot or undershoot the mark with shots to the green.

Similarly, even the most experienced player can be made to feel that the carry from the tee is most unreasonable when, in fact, it might be no more than the length of a medium-sized par-3 hole. They jump on the tee-shot, miss it badly through loss of composure and rhythm, and leave the scene loudly condemning the designer as a mean-minded jackass who should be locked-up.

One is slow to reveal all the secrets of design involved in the making of the links at The European Club. After all, part of the game is to have the player unravel the mystery for himself just like the detectives wrestle to solve crime mysteries on television!

One of the greatest design weapons is, of course, the wind which is ever present on linksland but from a different direction day-on-day and often changes a few times within the same day.

To maximise this factor great care has been taken to direct holes to every possible point of the compass and to balance a hole running east with a corresponding hole running west. The shape of the property allowed this to happen at Brittas Bay as, unlike the narrow strip effect at St. Andrews which forces the Old Course to run straight out and straight back, it runs far enough inland to accommodate long holes running to and from the sea as well as holes running along the coast. So, you will find the 415-yard eighth running due north and the 432-yard seventeenth running due south. The 466-yard tenth runs due east, straight at the sea, and the 477-yard eighteenth runs due west with its back to the sea. This pattern of balance repeats throughout the links in a way seldom found in dunesland and it is one of the main reasons why it takes multiple visits to understand the place as it varies in many ways each time that the wind veers to a new point.

Similar care has been taken to reward and to challenge the fader and the drawer of the golf ball. For example, a draw at the sixth will be threatened by the stream which hugs the left side of the green; and a fade will be similarly dangerous at the seventh as the same stream hugs that green on the right! The best chance of success rests with an ability to play a variety of shots.

That is how it should be, of course, in an age when technology threatens to reduce golf to a straight-line game. Hit it across everything from A to B and then take dead aim across all remaining hazards to C is the modern dictum. Careful course design can help keep the shotmaker in the race.

DROUGHT CRISIS 1995

It all tries to unravel in a long, hot Summer!

It is always fun to sit around and reminisce and all the more so when it is with a grand old champion such as the late Paddy Skerritt who hailed from Lahinch and was a winner on the European Tour in the 1960s. He was one of the nicest people ever and a great story teller as are so many people from his native place.

Our conversation in the clubhouse of The European Club, one evening when everyone else was gone and we were just enjoying watching the sun go down, turned to the matter of irrigation and fast running fairways and the good old days. Both of us tended towards romantic memories of when we were boys and everything was wonderful. There were snatches of lucidity, too, as we rambled along through the years.

My contribution to realism was a recollection of having hit a good drive down the first fairway at Rosses Point and being unable to find the ball under a canopy of daisies which, on their annual visit before weed controls became effective, grew just tall enough to close-in over the golf ball and hide it. It is impossible to forget the frustration of having to go back and play three off the tee and then face into another search in the fairway!

Skerritt was a bit taken aback by that until his memory cells began to function and he recalled the thrill of playing Lahinch when it was dry and crisp. Playing into the evening sun off the first tee after work the only way one could tell where the ball had gone was when it touched the fairway and sent up a little cloud of dust. Those were the days. His lovely round Irish face fairly glowed and radiated happiness as he spent a few minutes in the past.

Then we got down to brass tacks. None of this would be any good for the modern golfer who likes things, well, nice! Weeds are out and so are bare lies and smelly socks gathering dust in a corner of

Gary Player is remembered at the par-4 eleventh which dog-legs left around a high dune.

the locker-room. Today's player wouldn't understand the advice of the great old champion and golf-writer Horace Hutchinson who gave this putting tip - Get down behind the ball, keeping it between you and the hole, and select a particular daisy over which to putt. Times and standards have changed a lot and daisies on a putting green today would lead to big trouble for the greenkeeper.

The same goes for dried-out fairways that begin to crack and return to sand. This was okay in the 1950s when so few people played, maybe as few as four hundred games a week at a great place like Rosses Point, and the wear-and-tear was quite light. Now that so many people play it is important that the sward is kept healthy and able to withstand the traffic and recover from the abuse. Thin and frail just won't withstand today's demands.

One got a taste of this first-hand in 1995 when Ireland was caught in the warm embrace of drought from early May through to mid-October. Not a drop of rain fell for five months while the temperatures soared and fairly baked-out the fairways. This was a moment of crisis.

The European Club links was in lovely shape with velvet greens and fairways bordered by substantial roughs at the end of April. So one felt safe taking a well-earned busman's holiday by going three weeks early to the U.S. Open at Shinnecock Hills in order to play some golf with friends in Boston and New York. It was with disbelief that one received calls from home, mostly from oldest son Gerard, that our links was burning and the fairways virtually dying. It could not be.

A great shock was in store when we returned home to find that Gerard was correct. We were in crisis. We had irrigation to the tees and greens but, like the vast majority of Irish golf courses then and now, not on the fairways. All the fairways were crispy brown and sand had begun to show through in patches on some of them.

Our two big water tankers were pressed into use for two shifts daily and we bought thousands of yards of hose and had special sprinklers made on stands so that we could get water out onto those fairways. Hours were spent hauling those pipes around and praying for rain. Memories flooded back of the difficult early days when we didn't have automated irrigation on the greens.

Back then Gerard and I spent all night out watering those greens when it didn't rain. The drill was to tie three hoses onto the back of a motor car and drive to the first green where one hose was set-up with sprinklers and linked to the water-box nearby and switched on. Then proceed to the second green and set-up a hose and sprinklers but do not switch on. Go to the third green and repeat the set-up procedure. Back to the first green then to disconnect the hose there to move it to the fourth green and switch on the water at the second green en route. This leap-frogging to continue all around the links and fully occupy an eight hour shift from 8p.m. to 4a.m.

Not nice work. But it had to be done while we got into position to go to fully automatic irrigation. Besides, it happened only in Summer and there were times when it rained and we got to rejoin the human race and enjoy a good night's sleep.

The low point came one night when one reached the seventeenth green and parked the motor car with its lights pointing across it to where the water-box was set in a dip. Across the green in that beam of light one scuttled, with thoughts of a warm bed within the next hour, and over a knoll beyond and into the shadow filled dip which happened to be filled with water also as the result of a leaking valve!

Now, here was a strange position for a fellow described by a critical newspaper article that very day as a powerful developer. Up to one's butt in water and thinking suicidal thoughts as the realisation dawned that the hose plug-in was nine inches below one's feet. To go for it or not?

Total immersion was undertaken with the murderous thought that the first player to criticise that green that day or ever again would be a dead man!

So here we were again. After installing automatic irrigation to the greens and tees, just as these things go, we enjoyed a few years of lovely soft Summers giving one to wonder whether that investment had been really necessary. But now we were embroiled in a drought the likes of which had not been seen in Ireland in over one hundred years and there were just a few moments of black comedy to relieve the situation. Like the day that a party from Pine Valley arrived to play.

As everyone knows, Pine Valley is a superb place and widely regarded as one of the very best golf courses on earth. One had read about it but had never been there in the forty years that one had played golf. Until April 1995 when an invitation to play brought one scuttling from Augusta to Philadelphia.

Unfortunately, it rained all day and there were three temporary greens in play as ice storms had caused damage, even more so to nearby Merion, but a miserable day in heaven is magic nonetheless and it proved an unforgettable experience.

The fact that one's first visit to a classic place found it in less than perfect condition, an outside chance at a place that is said to be kept superbly almost always, was to prove a slight help in August when one was back at The European Club and unkempt and unshaven after several hours manning the hoses when a group of American players came off the links and one started to complain loudly of the state of the fairways. "Its a great course', he bellowed, 'but its in terrible condition". "Sorry, Sir,' one said, 'but we're in the middle of a drought".

"The place should be closed,' he responded. "The flaw with that,' all one could say, 'is that we mighn't be able to open again".

Somehow one happened to glance down at the timesheet and notice that a group from Pine Valley was playing that day. "Are you from Pine Valley, sir?', one asked. He confirmed that he was.

"The greatest course on earth,' one pressed on, 'and thrilled I was to play it in April". This surprised him as he examined the untidy figure in front of him and he enquired how I had got to play there.

The story of one's pilgrimage to Pine Valley was told without trying to hide one's disappointment at having had to play it in the rain and at a time when temporary greens were in play. "But I didn't complain,' one pressed home the advantage, 'because troubles visit us all. We just went in and enjoyed the snapper soup and came home very happy". Game, set and match. He vanished into the locker-room and, to his credit, an apology note arrived a few weeks later and he has become a regular visitor and a friend. Golfers have a bond.

It was a small victory in the middle of a war but not a real victory because one knew that one had fallen short of the mark. It was great to find that real golfers understood and accommodated the situation as did all our members who remained unfailingly supportive throughout the crisis with many of them seeking to volunteer to man the hoses! That was a gratifying but very humbling experience and the lesson has not been forgotten.

So it was with nothing short of elation that one welcomed the first rain of the season when it fell in the second week of October. The siege had been lifted and just in time to allow grass to be grown back before ground temperatures dropped for the Winter.

We had very little time to celebrate, however, before another crisis descended upon us with huge easterly storms driving the Irish Sea into the rocks beside the fifteenth hole and sending salty spray two hundred yards inland and killing the drought weakened fairway and green completely.

Luckily, we had a wonderful member named Maurice Cully, unfortunately soon to be ravaged by cancer, who had recently acquired an adjoining piece of dunesland and he agreed to let us lift sod from it to carry out repairs. It was a big job and it was bitterly cold and one judged wisely that this was a good time to stay outdoors working shoulder-to-shoulder with the greenkeepers who almost rebelled after a few days of the tough going but stayed loyal to the resident lunatic.

68

Visitors to The European Club are greeted by our dolmen and it creates quite a stir amongst the camera carrying fraternity as an ideal Celtic prop for a memorable group photograph. There are about one hundred dolmens in the Irish landscape and it is believed they were created between 3,000 and 2,000 B.C. as portal tombs for the most important people or as places of ritual. They were originally covered in earthen mounds with the capstone forming an entrance to the tomb.

The dolmen was chosen as the symbol of The European Club to symbolise Celtic permanence and the addition of a golf ball on top ties it into golf.

The cursing stone, above, is to be found along the tenth fairway. The idea was to rotate the seven small stones on top of the cursing stone in an anticlockwise fashion while imposing a spell or a curse on someone. However, if there was no just cause the curse would rebound on the curser!

THE DOLMEN
THE IRISH LANDSCAPE IS DOTTED WITH DOLMENS · BELIEVED TO BE NEOLITHIC BURIAL MARKERS

It was tough and bitterly cold going. But we got it done and opened for play in good order in 1996 and dedicated a gorge in the cliffs to the memory of our late friend and saviour - Cully's Gully. It is always pleasant to think of our old friend and one hopes that Cully's Gully is on the map to stay.

Now that we could lift our heads and look around one began to realise that the drought hadn't been confined to The European Club alone. Rob Armstrong, the veteran CBS news correspondent, produced a lovely book on Irish golf courses after a tour of the country in 1995 and his pictures showed brown fairways from coast-to-coast. The penny dropped. We had just come through an historic challenge to anyone involved in grass culture in Ireland.

The whole country was brown. Hopefully the likes will never be seen again but one wonders with all the talk of global warming.

The Irish climate is pretty ideal for grass growing in the main. It is a temperate climate without excesses of heat or cold and with golf playable all year through on the coastal links where frost is seldom a factor.   Snow does fall in Ireland but seldom stays more than a few days. We have had snow for just one half of a day since we opened for play and when it had melted pretty good by mid-morning our players went out using yellow golf balls and really enjoyed themselves.

At the other end of the spectrum we get one or two really warm and dry stretches, usually in May and again in July or August, each year and providing we keep the grass nicely alive through those we don't have to worry too much about water. That 1995 season was an exception.

That we weren't the worst hit soon became clear when Portmarnock Golf Club relinquished the right to host the Irish Open Championship of 1996. This was to one's benefit as the event was transferred to one's latest design, created in partnership with the late Tom Craddock, at Druid's Glen where it was to reside for four years. It is indeed a dark cloud that doesn't have a hole in it and it turned out that this cloud had a second hole!

On one of their always welcome visits for a chat about golf the Portmarnock veteran members John Fitzgibbon, who won the Irish Amateur Open back in 1955, and Paddy Kelleher consoled one with the information that their great links had suffered drought damage also and that they were about to spend an unspeakable sum of money installing a new irrigation system as a result. They suggested that one should buy Portmarnock's old system and expressed the view that any reasonable offer would be likely to be accepted.

Budgetary considerations, and the fact that only about five or six Irish courses had fairway irrigation at that time, meant that one had never really addressed the possibility of a fairway system. The fact that one was somewhat prejudiced against watering had a lot to do with the matter as well.

Indeed, when the Curragh Golf Club became the first Irish golf club to install pop-up watering to their greens in the mid-1960s one wrote in the Dublin "Evening Herald" that they were quite crazy introducing such silly American ideas to the Emerald Isle where our weather was ideal for producing grass without such sorcery. Now, about thirty years later, one was a convert.

The mind had been prepared by journeys in America where lovely grass was played upon even in the desert in Nevada and Arizona. What lovely golf they enjoy in those parts! Tucson was a particularly happy hunting ground and it was there one came into contact with tumbleweed as it bounced across the greens at Tucson National. All it lacked was John Wayne.

Even in the heat of Dubai they are growing lovely golf courses with desalinated water. This is the source of very positive thinking for the future, global warming or not, as The European Club links sits right on the edge of the sea. There is water from here to Australia to draw upon if the need arises and unless someone starts-up a "Save the Sea" campaign to thwart us.

So the mind was in position for a decision on more irrigation and the deal was done with Portmarnock and we were propelled into a new age. New pumps, miles of pipes and those sprinklers from Portmarnock helped us to bring our fairways to a new pitch of perfection. Despite the fact that all of the Portmarnock sprinklers have long since been retired we will never forget the kindness of the two wise men who came from one of the world's finest clubs to inspire a very important move.

One by one the Portmarnock sprinklers gave up the ghost. One should have known that there would be trouble in store with second-hand goods like that. But the positive thing was that one had been prompted to address the fairway irrigation issue and to commence the investment programme which was vital to our future.

No golf course can afford to let its course go to pot in drought times and it was pleasing to note that we were amongst the first ten Irish golf clubs to go with watering throughout the property. Not bad for a place reputed to be moving slowly. The fairways at The European Club have been excellent for many years now and this is thanks in no small way to our ability to control matters when drought conditions strike for eight or nine weeks each year. It doesn't take much to keep things healthy, we take care not to overdo the watering and just apply enough to keep the grass moving, but it would still be sheer hell if we had to go back to tankers and manual hosing.

LIFETIME APPROACH PAYS DIVIDENDS

Many Design Improvements Just Evolve

The fact that one spent almost thirty years working one's way, mentally and actually, towards The European Club and has spent twenty years so far living with it and developing it has resulted in a much better and more interesting links than would have been had one walked away after the first few years. Few places can have enjoyed the benefits of such a prolonged design and refine process.

There has been time to mature, both oneself as a designer and the place, and the game has changed so much. Quite apart from style and form the links is one of the very few on the planet which has the hazards placed correctly for today's play.

There has been time, too, to consider criticisms and the reactions of players and to make modifications where deemed prudent. The most outstanding example of this type of thing occurred at the eighteenth where the green is located in what was a mini-marsh when we started. It presented an opportunity to put a water hazard in front of the green and this was done in the form of a little lake.

Well, that proved controversial in the extreme as critic after critic went away and wrote nice things about the links but ended by bewailing the existence of that lake which they deemed had no place on a links.

This came as a shock and a disappointment. The lake was quite a feature and gave cause for lots of loud cheering and wailing on the eighteenth fairway as bets were won and lost at the very last moment as was the design intent. But the critics wailed louder. Something was going to have to happen.

Jean Van de Velde in the Barry Burn prompted the conversion of our pond at the eighteenth green (inset) into a burn.

But it took time to resolve. In fact, the position was pondered and the critics listened to for years before the design answer presented itself.

One did not want to give-up the water hazard. A shot over water is one of the most excruciating in golf. There is always doubt, nerve shredding questioning, when the ball is out there over the water and measuring glances first at the ball and then at the expressionless water only confuse and induce panic. Will it make it?

America is to be thanked for developing today's brilliantly bold water hazards and this is one of the best ideas ever to emerge from that fine country so why not embrace it when given the opportunity? What harm could there be in having a little bit of that? But the critics wailed and wailed.

There is never water on a links was the roar from the critics. How wrong they were. After all, the very first water hazard in golf wends its way across the first fairway at St. Andrews itself. But they didn't want to listen to that or take on board the fact that streams and burns come strongly into play at such famous links as Royal St. George's, Turnberry, County Sligo and Carnoustie! They just chipped away until a solution presented itself at Carnoustie in the British Open Championship of 1999.

Who could ever forget the climax to that Championship as Jean van de Velde had the title in his grasp coming to the last hole only to have his ball rebound off a grandstand into long rough from which he chopped into the Barry Burn.

It was sporting tragedy and drama of the highest order and an enriching moment for everyone who witnessed the Frenchman's poise and grace under the most severe stress.

It was the single most wonderful celebration, pardoning oneself to poor Mr de Velde, of water on a links and it caused a flash of inspiration leading to a solution to the problem at home on the eighteenth hole at The European Club. The lake was drained and filled-in. But one decided to hold onto the presence of water by converting the lake into a wriggling, squirming burn wending its way across the fairway in front of the green. Our own version of the Barry Burn.

One twist brought it up the fairway to exactly where the shore of the lake used to be; two other twists, and this is the fun part, brought it five yards closer to the putting surface than the lake had been. The surrounding ground either tilts gently towards the burn or is flat. Nothing was done to stop balls running into the water as this is the business of the player alone.

It has to be admitted that the burn looks a lot nicer than the lake. With its sleepered face presenting a writhing and menacing challenge to the mental and physical fibre of the player it is all that one would have hoped for in the matter of last hole torment. One got to hold one's water and yet silence the critics while proving that their concern is not with the presence of water but with the shape of it! It was twelve years after the turning of the first sod for the links that the lake issue was resolved on the eighteenth.   If one hadn't stayed on the premises all those years this design wrinkle would not have been teased-out so carefully.   There is no question but that working and reworking thoughts moves one towards better design situations so it is with increasing interest and excitement that one faces into one's third decade of design and presentation challenges at The European Club.

Another lovely result of what could be termed prolonged designing is to be found at the twelfth green which is quite a monster measuring 127-yards from front to back. How this came to be is quite a story in itself. This hole was designed originally as a classic par-4 of 422-yards with the fairway skirting the beach on the right and bending gently towards a beautifully contoured green with a dip in front. It looked good and it played good.

The thirteenth tee was to the right of that green, almost on the beach, and the tee-shot was up along the beach to the north.   That, too, played very good.

The problem was that there was a lovely, natural greensite up in the dunes to the left of the twelfth fairway and it was eating away at the mind.   It was just too good to leave unused but it couldn't be worked into an 18-hole plan yielding two loops of nine-holes returning to the clubhouse at greens nine and eighteen.   Things fell into place when the decision was made to build two extra par-3s with one of them using this site for what became known as hole 12a.

Now the player exited the twelfth green on the inland side to play 12a. So the tee for the thirteenth was moved to that side also and a new portion of fairway was built to run downhill towards the beach and cascade into the second half of the old thirteenth fairway with lovely backdrop views of the Irish Sea.   It worked perfectly and added a great deal of extra strategy to the thirteenth as well as freeing-up the first half of the old thirteenth fairway behind the twelfth green.

This was a most attractive design bonus as it allowed not alone for an extension of the twelfth hole but a movement of the green towards the beach thus introducing the option of longer and more dangerous shots in keeping with the way the game was going. So it was with mounting excitement that work got underway building that new green which would bring the twelfth up to 507-yards. Then the doubts flooded in.

The existing twelfth green was so perfect. How could one abandon it? Could one bear seeing players ripping divots out of it once it became merely a part of the fairway approach to the new green? The answers were no and no.

So it was resolved to simply join the old green and the new green together by creating one hugely long green! It was a case of eating your cake and keeping it! A visit was paid to St. Andrews to double-check the widths of their double greens and the decision taken to make our new single twelfth green seven yards longer than their widest double. No point in being second in a fun-filled world.

Behind all the fun one did not lose sight of the underlying serious design elements. Fun and design and intrigue should go together in golf and the new green was intriguing in many ways. Not least, it introduced the possibility of a marvellous three-putt as opposed to the normally disappointing version of that dark art.

If a weak or overhit approach, depending on pin position, left a putt of 100-yards it would be quite an achievement to get down in two putts and this didn't remove the possibility of nervous short putts which could arise after a great fairway approach or a weak first putt. One had to spend an exasperating hour explaining this to a fellow who proclaimed that the long green took the emphasis off short putts. "Look,' he was told, 'a big green contains big putts and little ones; but a small green offers only small putts". It took a long time for him to get his head around it.

Obviously, it will take a bad approach to leave a hugely long putt. Or a hugely long chip from off the fringe and they are almost as difficult to judge, being so unfamiliar to people, as those shots across water. Unfamiliar country unsettles the modern golfer like nobody's business. Which raises another great point concerning our long green.

Standing at the 150-yard marker on the fairway today's play by the numbers man is in trouble. If the pin is far away from the middle of the green he has some serious problems unless he is willing to go back to the old ways of doing a little math and playing with a dash of feel and intuition.

We were the first in, thanks to this green, with a par-4 of over 500-yards. At the front pin position the hole played par-4 of 412-yards and at the back it played par-4 at 515-yards! Now the 500-yard par-4 is much in vogue in tournament play and we have been overtaken.

One downside of the long green is that it takes a lot of maintenance and the greenkeepers never like it when it comes their turn to mow it with a walk behind machine as it involves a walk of 1.5-miles! There are no fat men on our staff.

That the long green adds an entertaining new dimension to the game is borne out by watching the reactions of players of all standards.   Nick Faldo came for a visit and spent a good while walking around it and muttering to the effect that it is a neat idea.   Behind the stern facade one detected the heart of a golfing boy.

The same happened when Tiger Woods played with David Duval, Mark O'Meara and Scott McCarron. Tiger proved that he loves the game just like us ordinary mortals when he paced around on the green and then insisted that they all play some ultra-long putts from the very front edge to the very back pin position. At that moment he became my hero.

It is a happy day when one strikes a common chord with the best player in the world.   It is happy, too, when day after day one sees groups of holidaying golfers trying big putts up and down that green after their play of the hole. The laughter and the banter that goes on certifies it as a winner.

The same process of evolution attached to the development of the figure-eight green at the thirteenth with a bunker tucked deeply into the central fold at the back. The seaside portion of this green constitutes the original green. A Winter storm in the early days chewed away the beach in a sheer drop of ten feet right to the edge of the green and it looked as if the next storm would finish the job.

Part of the solution was to build a new green further in from the beach and have it ready in case a retreat became necessary in front of an attacking sea. It would be good to have a Winter green, or a rest green, in any case. From there it was an easy step to link the two greens to produce a unique and lovely golfing situation.

In the midst of all this work, while we were installing a rock armour defence between what was left of the beach and the green, a fellow turned-up and started to take pictures of the beach and the green. When approached he expressed the view that we were destroying a nesting ground for the tern. He left when it was pointed-out in no uncertain terms that any terns who had been nesting on the beach the week previous had lost their nests when the beach had been swept away. Nature has been good since then and restored the beach and the golfers and the terns co-exist happily.

So the process continues. A substantial notebook is maintained to store the myriad of design ideas which arise as one works on the links and plays on it and watches players of all levels play on it. It would be foolish to run out and implement them all at once. That would disrupt play too much and, in any case, it is better to leave each idea lie about for awhile and see does it mature into a fine wine or turn to vinegar.

But every year there have been improvements and every year there will be improvements.

THE COURSE RANKINGS

A controversial but very valuable institution.

International attention has focused on The European Club from the very start with all the relevant rankings of golf courses since the mid-1990s featuring our links at Brittas Bay.

They have placed it in Ireland's Top-5 regularly, they have placed it in Britain & Ireland's Top-25 regularly and they have voted it into the World's Top-100 in the three most recent polls.

Significantly, when the international rankings run by Golf World and Golf Monthly in Britain and by GOLF and Golf Digest in America are analysed it emerges that The European Club is always amongst Ireland's top six courses along with Royal County Down, Royal Portrush, Ballybunion, Lahinch and Portmarnock.

That would have been a very satisfactory target to aim at when we started to build The European Club back in 1987 and it is gratifying when so many people place us in such company.

A variation on the theme happened when GOLF magazine headed a consortium of twelve golf publications worldwide to name the 500 Greatest Holes in the World at the year 2000. They picked three holes from The European Club with the par-4 seventh being nominated one of the World's 100 Greatest Holes. The par-5 thirteenth and par-3 fourteenth were included in the 500 Greatest.

This is taken as a substantial endorsement of our links. Much the same as the producer of fine literature or of stunning art would be relieved and gratified to receive the approval of his public and of the critics one is pleased to find that our links is well regarded.

To be mentioned in the rankings at all is wonderful. To be mentioned in all of the rankings and almost invariably in a higher position than before is even more wonderful as it would suggest that different judging panels in different countries agree that our links is good.

The local Irish rankings place us high in the order of things. We have not been lower than seventh

This is just a corner of the twelfth green which is the longest in the world at 127-yards deep from front to back.

best in the country since we made our debut in 1994 and as high as second by 2005. The Irish rankings given to us in three polls by the now defunct Irish Golf Institute and latterly in two polls by Golf Digest Ireland are seventh, sixth, fifth, second and fifth.

Such praise from one's nearest neighbours is most welcome as they are most familiar with the Irish courses and are in a prime position to assess their relative merits. This has given one a major boost as the efforts are put in to make the links ever better with the simple objective of attempting to become the most perfect of them all. That is not meant to be big-headed but an honest mission statement.

Now, one is aware of the criticisms levelled at the rankings. One is in agreement with some of these criticisms as one does not believe that it is possible to number the courses 1-to-20 or 1-to-100 in a strict numerical order of merit.

The distinctions are too fine between courses ranked close to each other for that to be scientific. But one does believe that, with some exceptions here and there, the rankings do a great job in bundling the courses on a merit basis.

By this one means that the courses ranked 81-to-100 on any of these lists would look strangely out of place if moved en bloc into positions 1-to-20; and those ranked 1-to-20 would feel seriously maligned if moved en bloc to positions 81-to-100.

It would be more extreme if someone came along and threw away the Top-100 on any of these rankings and sought to replace them with totally different courses. The rankings are not perfect but they are pretty good.

The judges by and large know a great deal about golf courses, most of them having devoted their lives to the game, and their collective wisdom seems accurate to about a 90%-plus factor. To those who say that there is no way to judge the merits of golf courses one would have to say- "Rubbish."

It is just as valid to make judgements on the artistic, sporting and functional merits of golf courses as it is to do so on any other form of architecture or artistic endeavour.

To say otherwise is to go in the direction of saying that golf course architecture is a haphazard and meaningless exercise not worthy of thought and not capable of being assessed.

It is one's belief that golf architecture has become a discipline finely balanced between art and science and that it is possible to distinguish clearly between good, indifferent and bad. The rankings help to focus many minds in this matter.

Certainly, since rankings were started in Ireland by the Irish Golf Institute in the early-1990s the

The fourteenth is a terrific par-3 of 195-yards across a valley. It is rated one of the 500 Greatest Golf Holes in the World.

Irish golf clubs have displayed a much heightened awareness of course detail and presentation. Course improvements are continuously afoot right across the country.

More importantly, vitally so, the rankings give every golf course an opportunity of being considered on its merits. How, otherwise, is a new golf course in the ownership of a normal person or normal club to come to be recognised widely on its merits against those venues which have the advantage of huge marketing budgets and/or are swathed in history?

No new course can manufacture instant history to compete for romantic laurels with the likes of St. Andrews, Augusta or Shinnecock. The promoters will be dead long before their creations join such venerable ranks. History has to make itself at its own pace. So, the newly created places under fifty years old have to doff the cap to the senior citizens while competing for attention.

Anyone who thinks that there is anything wrong with such competition and suggests that the old places are not promoting themselves needs to waken-up. Augusta has the Masters to showcase itself annually, St. Andrews has the (British) Open at regular intervals, and the Shinnecocks and Pebble Beaches know the value of staging the U.S. Open at intervals.

Which is all very good except when some of the older courses seek to establish or perpetuate an aura of superiority based more on age than fact. Just as old cars and old planes become museum pieces so it is with old golf courses unless they are kept up to date. There are more than a few dated courses holding high rankings on reputation rather than modern architectural merit.

The ultimate test of a golf course has to be how capable it is of withstanding the skills of the great players of the present age.

Being full of atmosphere, being exclusive, having a great history will not have much to do with the basic questions - is it a great test of the game and is it a beautiful work of landscape art?

To hold badly out-dated courses high in the rankings at the cost of the today's master works of course design is to do a disservice to the best modernists who have made a deep study of the elements that comprise a modern golf course, of the recognised great venues and of the great performances of the best players of today before undertaking the creation of the new classic golf courses.

Of course, care must be taken not to be swayed unduly by developers who spend fortunes in an effort to dress up mutton as lamb. They seek to impress with palatial facilities and extravagant gardens. Many even sponsor tournaments, brazenly claiming then that they were the chosen venue, in an effort to create an aura of substance.

This is where the rankings help introduce balance once more. Not everyone has the finances or the inclination to compete head-on with the big spending places whether they be from the new school or the old. The rankings alone afford the opportunity for objective thinking on the intrinsic merits of golf courses.

Rankings are here to stay and they have a valid function to perform as they are followed eagerly by devotees of the game, by golf architects and by course owners all of whom have to make renewed efforts to define what makes a great golf course.

The underlying mathematics changed drastically in the 1990s with the ball flying so far that an elite player can now expect to cover something like 4,200-yards with just fourteen tee-shots!

That leaves him with fifty-four strokes to complete the journey around what is left of the course for a score of 68. Even a big course of 7,200-yards has been reduced to 3,000-yards remaining, or an average of just 166-yards per hole, with a true championship par figure of 68!

It is for this reason that there have been a number of 59s in tournaments in recent years. It is just amazing that there have not been more.

It is for this reason also that some of the best sports psychologists have begun to encourage their star customers to take aim at 54 as the ideal golf score!

Just as surely as the sub-four-minute mile became old hat in athletics once the way was shown the game of tournament golf is moving inexorably into uncharted waters.

Shades of Ben Hogan wakening-up in a cold sweat after dreaming of a round of seventeen ones and a two. Perfection had eluded him when he took a two! But he had achieved a position where it was possible to dream the dreams.

It is the task of the golf manufacturers and of the top players to assault the golf course and seek to tear it to shreds. It is left to the golf course architect, who is home alone on guard duty, to present design solutions to test the players' nerves just as much as their brawn while leaving plenty of room for the expression of skills.

The golfing predator must not be denied his prey if he is strong enough of mind and body. But, just as in bull-fighting, the hunted and taunted must not lose every contest or it will become so boring! The golf course must fight back. The links at The European Club is prepared to answer any imaginable challenge from player and technology for years to come. That is the chosen basis of our life in golf while ensuring that the sane and modest golfer will enjoy a game off his own tees.

WORLD'S GREATEST GOLF HOLES

Three of ours are included in the honours!

A most entertaining exercise was undertaken in 1999 by an alliance of twelve golf magazines worldwide.* They came together to see whether they could nominate "The World's 500 Greatest Golf Holes" at the turn of the millennium.

GOLF magazine of the U.S.A. spearheaded the exercise which saw each magazine invite its readers to nominate their best golf holes, some of the magazines had their own experts give their views also, and the final adjudication took place at a summit meeting of the editors at the 1999 (British) Open Championship at Carnoustie where Sir Michael Bonallack, then secretary of the R&A, and U.S.G.A. executive director David Fay joined in the stimulating process.

They selected 125 par-3 holes, 125 par-5 holes and 250 par-4 holes to yield a perfect overall par for the millennium of 2000!

The holes chosen were all quite delightful, many of them amongst the most famous in the world, and there was little doubt but that a great many wonderful golf courses could be produced by blending the various selected holes together in different combinations.

It was a thrill to discover that three holes from The European Club had been included and there were more thrills when a subsequent exercise elevated our par-4 seventh into the "The World's 100 Greatest Golf Holes" and also into a list of the eighteen "Best Holes Designed Since 1970"!

Our par-5 thirteenth and par-3 fourteenth were named as amongst "The World's 500 Greatest Golf Holes" to round-off an overwhelming recognition of the links at Brittas Bay as very few venues had three holes included on the list.

The seventh hole at The European Club is terrible beauty and was named as one of the World's 100 Greatest Golf Holes.

The seventh hole at The European Club is the Handicap Index 1 hole on the links as it measures a monstrous 470-yards with trouble everywhere to be found except on tee, fairway and green.

A small river runs in front of the tees and hugs the fairway and the green all the way on the right. A golfer doesn't want to have anything to do with that other than to look admiringly beyond the river and up a wild, conserved valley which gives the hole a marvellous setting and sense of solitude.

Meanwhile, on the left of the hole is jungle and a reed-filled marsh protrudes into the fairway 300-yards from the championship tee. The player needs to take the risk of getting his drive up into the area of the marsh or increase the difficulties associated with the second shot.

Many are fooled into going with an iron for safety and into hitting down the left side for the same reason. Of course, having gone left off the tee one must now hit back across the green towards the river. Once on the fairway the reeds dominate life. To the player on the left of the fairway it looks as though the reeds run all the way to the green and that a gigantic hit is required to carry them. In fact, the reeds run only from yard-300 to yard-405 and most golfers should be capable of having their ball airborne for those vital 105-yards (bearing in mind that the base measurements are from the championship tees and those going from the medal tees may subtract 21-yards from these numbers) on either their second or third shots.

But fear and self-doubt can take hold, especially as the awareness of the river on the right never goes away, and many people self destruct here. This is clearly a hole where the handicap player should keep in mind that he is in receipt of a stroke from the card. But greed combined with fear deadens the brain of normally very astute players.

The seventh hole at The European Club is what one likes to term a "set piece" hole. By this is meant a hole which demands two good strokes in succession to set-up par or better. Other holes may be similar to the examination paper which offers multiple choice questions, e.g. answer A, B or C. But the set-piece hole asks one to answer a definite question or fail.

In the context of a 72-hole tournament this type of hole becomes crucial as the player has to pass the test four times. Deliver now or fail. Only the most controlled and skilled players can survive and that is as it should be at tournament level.

The European Club's par-5 thirteenth hole was named as one of "The World's 500 Greatest Holes" and was also identified as one of "The World's Eighteen Best Ocean Holes."

This is an heroic hole of 596-yards which gave Tiger Woods great pleasure on his visit in 2002 as he

The thirteenth is a par-5 of 596-yards and Tiger Woods enjoyed playing a driver off the deck to gain the front edge in two.

smashed driver off the tee high in the dunes and took the driver again for his second into the wind and nailed it beautifully, dead on line for the flag, to one pace off the front edge. An easy birdie after two magnificent blows.

The high tee has meaning. It means that the ball is higher in the air than one might like on a windy day beside the sea. A real tester of a shot to a terraced fairway which drops rapidly to the level of the beach and runs parallel to the sea for the last 260-yards of the journey.

Built into the second shot is one of my favourite design secrets: The deadly relationship between the angle of desire and the angle of disaster. This works best on this hole when the flag is on the right or seaward side of the green and the good and greedy player is tempted to do a Tiger on it and go for the target in two. This requires a shot which is moving at an angle off-centre, because the second half of the fairway dog-legs slightly left, and towards the beach.

In this situation it takes just a slightly imperfect shot to open further that angle to the right and send the ball onto the beach. It is quite amazing how quickly attraction can lead to disaster.

When the wind is from the west the danger is compounded as the devil's wings are given added frantic life as they waft that ball towards the Irish Sea. When players complain about their ball going onto the beach here, or at the equally cunning twelfth hole, they get scant sympathy at the clubhouse and can be given the irrefutable rebuke - "You didn't just miss a fairway; you managed to miss an entire country by going on the beach!"

After finishing play on the thirteenth the players have to climb a short but stiff path to the tee of the par-3 fourteenth. This short climb causes the body to change a gear approaching one of the testiest shots of the day and the wise players will take a few moments to compose themselves as they survey the test ahead.

What a lovely place this is to take a breather. The thirteenth lies below along the beach and the sea; look to the left and the eye falls upon the magnificent fifteenth hole as it climbs up onto the rocks of Mizen Head where white foam often lashes the inveterate Winter golfer; and inland is the deep valley which houses the seventeenth hole. It takes an effort to concentrate on the golf amidst such stunning beauty.

The fourteenth was named as one of "The World's 500 Greatest Golf Holes" and just why this was so will be appreciated by a player standing on the elevated championship tee and looking 195-yards across a rough-filled valley to a well bunkered plateau green which looks tiny.

88

This is a high octane situation towards the end of a round. The eye has to focus on those bunkers as much as on the green. One to the left, one at the back and huge cavern lined with sleepers up the right edge. The tightest pin position is in the back right corner of the green as the flag now sits on a tiny nose of land protruding between the back and right bunkers. Only a powerful and precise blow will get the player close enough for a good shot at birdie. It is a daunting challenge.

The front pin positions are no gifts, either, as they bring the two side bunkers into play and any shot going long involves a dangerous downhill putt to follow.

It has to be admitted that it was exciting having three of our golf holes honoured by a worldwide jury by inclusion amongst "The World's 500 Greatest Golf Holes". All the more so when one has the belief that there are several more holes of equal merit on the links.

In this respect, quite a debate could be stirred-up concerning the relative merits of the golf holes throughout the links. It is said that beauty is in the eye of the beholder but our experience at The European Club has been that rare beauty, like that found at many points on our links, is beheld by all. Certainly, a day never passes without unsolicited compliments being offered by gasping players, tired after an epic trip through one of the most exacting and exciting games of their lives, to the effect that this hole or that is the most beautiful that they have ever seen.

There is no questioning, either, the requirement for a thrill or fear factor to waken the latent hunter within every golfer. Standing on tees like hole seven at The European Club is just about as good as it gets in this regard. The delivery of a good stroke is never more rewarding than when death awaits a bad stroke. Even to fail in these situations is no shame. To attempt an heroic deed is invigorating and stimulating in itself.

The great golf hole has to be correctly balanced and presented to provide valid golf for all players (assuming that they have the wisdom to play off the tees that suit their games). The questions must be seen clearly. A challenge must be presented automatically, even sub-consciously, to the primeval human instincts of pride and bravado. Above all it must be fair. The test must be one with a realistically available solution.

At The European Club we seek all of this and more on every hole.

* The twelve magazines which took part in "The World's 500 Greatest Golf Holes" exercise were- Andalucia Golf (Spain/Portugal), Asian Golfer (Far East), Buenos Aires Times (South America), The Compleat Golfer (South Africa), Golf Europeen (France), Golf Magazine Australia, Golf Magazine (U.S.A.), Golf Monthly (Britain), Il Mondo Del Golf (Italy), Score (Canada), Svensk Golf (Sweden) and Wirtschafts Woche (Germany).

CHASING PERFECTION

Small land acquisitions allow huge improvements!

Small things matter a great deal when perfection is the goal and good is not good enough when excellence is attainable.

This is the underlying philosophy which has driven one's efforts to make the links of The European Club a truly outstanding place to play golf.

No Winter has been allowed to pass without a vigorous programme of improvements to the links. A ledger of ideas is maintained regarding possible future improvements to be approached on a phased basis so as to allow golf to continue comfortably while work is progressing. That ledger is constantly updated and priorities reviewed.

Similarly, a number of land acquisitions were undertaken after the links had been designed in order to make improvements possible and, in the nature of these things, each purchase was more expensive than the last as it was known that one was interested.

Two small but hugely significant patches of ground helped to improve holes seven and sixteen very dramatically and that eased the pain of having to pay well above the odds for them. The money is long gone and forgotten but the improvements to those holes give pleasure every time they are looked at or thought about.

The problem at the seventh on opening day was that the tee was squashed very close between the par-3 sixth and the stream to the left of it. This was a bit dangerous and it eliminated the possibility of introducing a new back tee at the seventh.

Now, if a sliver of ground could be acquired on the far side of the stream the tee for the seventh could be moved over there and the sixth hole would be much more spacious.

It would also allow a new back-tee to be introduced on the seventh and the creation of a lovely path

A fine gathering bunker at the right of the third green. The fairway slopes towards it and two bunkers on the left guide play that way!

from the sixth green across a bridge, along the far shore of the stream past the new tees and back over another bridge onto the seventh fairway. It would be lovely and much better golf.

The snag was that the neighbouring landowner was reluctant to sell as he had worries about access to the stream for water for his cattle. It took seven years of waiting for him to change his mind and do a deal. What a happy day that was, despite the need to pay well above market value for the land, and one was grateful to the neighbour for allowing one to improve the links so much.

Now the sixth hole had a space all its own and the new tees for the seventh transformed that hole so much that it was ultimately to be named as one of the 100 Greatest Golf Holes in the World!

The drive was now aimed over the stream, which snaked from left to right in front of the tees, to a fairway which was much more visible than before. The new alignment also meant that the player was now required to hit a straight tee-shot, one of the rarest of animals when needed under pressure, or go left on the fairway creating an awkward angle back to the green.

Better still, a new championship tee could be introduced stretching the hole by 37-yards to a modern par-4 classic length of 470-yards. The view from that tee is magnificent and never fails to excite a player who is willing to take a chance at delivering a worldclass shot.

Meantime, life was much more dramatic at the other end of the property at hole sixteen. There was a problem with this tee-shot from the start as a boundary fence jutted into the edge of the fairway at the corner of the dog-leg right. That fence looked ugly and it was difficult to maintain as golfers were constantly scrambling over it in pursuit of their golf balls.

Things got more complicated when the adjoining farm changed hands and the new owner set about transforming it into an airfield. To say that one was shell-shocked at the idea of a noisey airfield next door, in a place which had been a haven of tranquillity from the beginning of time, is to understate the case.

It got worse. Because when the airfield opened for business they started to give flying lessons which entailed planes circling around the links for eight and nine hours many days. It was a mad house as seen through the eyes of a golfer.

Pleas to go fly their planes elsewhere for part of each day, at least, failed to get a result. So, when the airfield applied for planning permission to retain their facility one had, much against one's wishes, no choice but to appeal the matter. The decision was to restrict the airfield to a private one and this helped a little but also inflicted an injury on our neighbour.

92

Understandably, this created a great deal of tension and our neighbour threatened to bring us to law if golf balls continued to go over the boundary fence to the right of the sixteenth fairway. Now, that was open farmland and the golf balls did not create a hazard to man or beast. But there was no disputing the fact that golf balls were entering his lands and that trespass was happening.

In all the circumstances things looked bleak.

Fairways fifteen and sixteen had just enough space to pass each other, parallel in opposite directions, up onto and back off Mizen Head while allowing an adequate safety margin between them. To move fairway sixteen to the left would create danger. It looked as if there would be nothing for it but to reduce hole sixteen to a par-3.

Acting against legal advice, but depending on one's basic belief in the decency of people at large, one paid a visit to the neighbour and asked for a meeting. He was gruff but agreed to talk.

My hands were raised in surrender. We had had our differences and I was sorry to have hurt him. My golfers and their golf balls were, indeed, trespassing on his lands and I was sorry and agreed that I would have to rectify that matter. One explained fully the difficulties faced on our side of the fence and asked whether he would in any way consider helping one with the only other solution possible: Would he sell the piece of land onto which those errant golf balls were going?

The response was positive. He named a high price. But he showed great humanity and decency in opening the door for a peaceful solution and one which was to enhance the golf links greatly.

One will never forget that transaction or cease being grateful to a fine man. It was a pleasure to deal with a gentleman with whom one could have differences and yet conduct business without having to have recourse to law.

Right away that ugly fence disappeared from the dog-leg on hole sixteen. A big bunker appeared at the spot where the apex of the fence had abutted the fairway and rough was allowed to grow behind it to preserve the original playing characteristics of the hole.

A few years later the airfield ceased to operate and the lands changed hands once more. One was fortunate to have hole sixteen sorted-out before that happened even though the whole situation looked quite bleak at the time. These traumas and dramas never impacted on the golfers who joined the club or who visited as guests. Everything was calm and pleasant at the front of the house and the players never knew the trouble they were causing by sending golf balls over that fence and going after them. Today's golfers enjoy a fine and good-looking golf hole not knowing that it was once a problem child!

HONOURING HEROES

Naming holes to honour great champions.

A consuming passion for golf was the driving force behind the foundation of The Eurpean Club. The need to create a place where one could play whenever the spirit moved in that direction or just loll about and think about golf, about life, and about golf again.

Of course, when thinking about golf the mind would be filled with images of the great moments and personalities of championship play and so it seemed appropriate to introduce to the links reminders of those great people and events. Reminders which would serve to focus players' minds on such pure golfing thoughts as they joined us for a game.

It seemed natural to share the joys of the way ahead with some of the greatest champions the game has known. To share the moment of creation of a new links with men who, surely, had loved this game with the same intensity.

Why not write to them and ask permission to name holes on our links in their honour? Further, ask them to describe the type of golf hole which they would like to have named for them.

It was a presumptuous move and it could have been mistaken as commercially inspired. These thoughts never occurred as the letters were written. The land was still in a wild and raw state - but the vision was complete.

This would be a fine links one day and what could be nicer than to have one's fledgling golf course grow into a loving memorial to the greatness of the men whose stories and achievements had provided much of the inspiration for it?

Innocently, but properly, a standard was set.

Only those who had won more than one major championship would be invited to allow a golf hole to be named in their honour.

Gene Sarazen and Sam Snead have their memories enshrined on holes fourteen and four.

Only men whose memory would survive the harsh amnesia of history, and whose sportsmanship was unquestioned, would be invited.

Two exceptions were made to these strict guidelines in order to honour a dear friend Fred Daly, who was Ireland's only winner of a major title by virtue of his win in the (British) Open at Hoylake in 1947, and to name our main putting green in honour of Harry Bradshaw.

We had travelled together a good deal in latter years as part of my business involved the promotion of pro-am tournaments and exhibitions and one of my favourite ploys was to have Daly, Harry Bradshaw and Henry Cotton give a clinic and they appreciated the fees which made the prize-monies they had won in their primes look puny.

It would not have been right to have left Bradshaw off the honours list. He lost the 1949 (British) Open at Royal St.George's only in a playoff with Bobby Locke after dropping a shot in real-time by playing a ball from inside a broken beer bottle. He was one of the greatest putters who ever lived, a member of the "hit 'n' hark" school and he loved the idea of his own putting green.

It was no surprise that Daly accepted the invitation with alacrity, also. He wrote - "Of course I am priviliged to have a hole named in my honour at Brittas Bay. Might I suggest a good driving hole, with a dog-leg right or left, which calls for accuracy off the tee. Throughout my golfing career that was the sort of hole I enjoyed most."

Easy. It had to be the lovely par-4 eighth hole for Fred Daly!

Henry Cotton, who had been a hero since boyhood, was next on the list. He had invited one to be his partner in course design after the 1980 Open at Muirfield where we had shared some happy moments. Sipping tea in the clubhouse with the great old champion was a revelation as everyone stopped to say hello to Henry and his Irish friend. Willie Whitelaw, deputy prime minister at the time, and actor Christopher Lee were two of the most entertaining companions we enjoyed that day.

The conversation turned to money, as it does with professionals, and we marvelled at the fact that the winner that week would receive £25,000. An astronomical sum when measured against the £100 which Cotton had received for each his first two wins in 1934 and 1937 and the £150 he received for his third win in 1948.

Nor had he made a £-million in endorsements. "In those circumstances,' one asked, 'what was the biggest benefit arising from those three wins?" The reply was a surprise - "Never having to buy lunch ever again."

Old friends Henry Cotton and Fred Daly, both of them friends of The European Club, have holes fifteen and eight named for them.

Anyway, one thing led to another, and when talk turned to sponsorship I offered to help and went to the tented village to meet Nat Rosasco of Northwestern Golf of Chicago, the biggest producer of golf clubs in the world at that time, to ask whether he would like to make use of the Henry Cotton name. Within the hour one had made the introductions and a deal was done.

Back in the clubhouse Cotton, now as content as a cat with cream, asked what he owed one for the service just performed. "Well,' one said, 'you have spent about 70-years sowing the seeds for this moment and I have spent two hours on it. So, a glass of lemonade will see us square."

His professionalism shone through as he accepted that with a simple smile. But he showed his gratitude the following week with a written invitation to be his partner in golf course design. Sadly, all we got to do was talk design as his health declined.

He was proud to accept the idea of having a hole named in his honour. His choice - "...a golf hole open to the sea breezes and demanding precision and a steady nerve in the shot to the green." This described the cliff-top fifteenth hole to perfection and so it is dedicated to an old friend.

It was at Royal Troon in 1982, while playing a ceremonial round in the Open with Fred Daly and Bobby Locke, that Gene Sarazen made a memorable hole-in-one at the famous Postage Stamp hole at age 71. Next day, he holed from a bunker for a birdie-2 at the same hole!

We met soon after that when one wandered accidentally into the Champions' Room at Augusta National. Instead of having one ejected he waved towards a chair near his and engaged one in conversation. This provided the basis for a later magazine tribute to Sarazen which one headlined "Gentleman Gene."Somehow that magazine found its way to Sarazen's home in Florida and, within weeks, a lovely handwritten letter of appreciation arrived. We became penfriends from then and he was always a delight to meet.

He understood the background to the invitation to have a hole named in his honour and wrote - "Its fine with me. I'd like a par-3 hole." We have named the fourteenth hole in his honour.

Another smashing rsponse was received from the legendary Byron Nelson who was such a lovely person to everyone he met. His feat in winning eleven tournaments in a row, and eighteen in all, in the 1945 season will never be equalled.

This man, the winner of a U.S. Open, two US PGA titles and two Masters sat down the day after the Byron Nelson Classic of 1989 and wrote:-

"I am honored that you wish to name a hole on your golf course for me. You have put me in very distinguished company, indeed. As for the type of golf hole that I enjoy playing, it would be either a par-3 that would require a long iron to the green, or else a par-4 or a par-5 that would have the same requirement to reach the green. I used to do rather well with those."

Indeed, he used to nail those irons to the flag and it was decided to dedicate the eighteenth, a par-4 of 477-yards, to this great Texan.

Arnold Palmer, who has to be one of the most affable of all superstars, responded positively as well but left the choice of golf hole to The European Club. He wrote- "I would be flattered to have a hole at your new course named in my honor. I would not have any particular preference as to the type of hole you would choose. Please let me know what you decide."

This was an automatic selection. Hole seven, the Handicap Index 1 hole, had to be the Arnold Palmer hole because here is a hole that requires the player to be brave and positive.... just like the young Arnold Palmer. We know that he is delighted that his golf hole has gone on to be selected as one of the 100 Greatest Golf Holes in the World!

Billy Casper was another great hero for golfers worldwide through the 1960s and 1970s. He was one of the greatest putters of all-time and his letter of acceptance through his manager reflected this: "Because of Mr. Casper's great success attributed to his unique putting style, I am requesting that a hole be named in his honor that contains a putting green with beautiful character. Aesthetics as well as playing ability is what appeals to Billy Casper."

We nominated hole twelve, a par-4 of 459-yards down by the beach, as the Casper hole and it is no coincidence that the green on this hole has since become one of the most remarkable greens in all of golf. It measures 127-yards from front to back and is the longest green in the world, longer as a single green than the widest double-green to be found at St. Andrews.

It is also a superb place to spend a few minutes of one's life. The twelfth hole runs in a valley between the high dunes and the beach and the green has been raised just enough that a golfer can see out over the foredunes to the sea. The hole is isolated from the rest of the links inland, a sort of hidden land in its own right, and it is a lovely place to dawdle at quiet times and admire the land, the sea and the sky in all their varied moods and interactions.

Gary Player Peter Thomson, Sam Snead and Tony Jacklin all responded positively to the idea of having holes named in their honour. It could be argued that Peter Thomson was one of the very last great players to run the ball as often as possible in links conditions. He was a superb manager of the

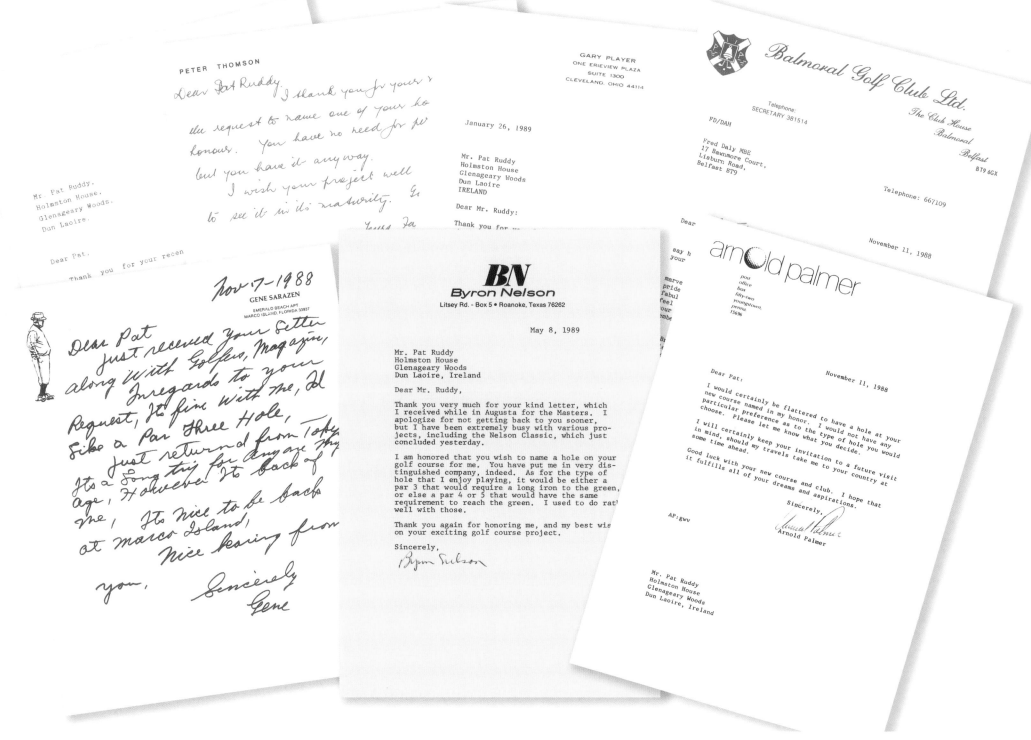

Some of the letters received from the old champions giving permission to name holes in their honour.

golf course and of himself and he could always see ways to bounce the ball home when others could not. One took care to name the fifth hole after him as it permits the low-flying approach shot.

Lee Trevino has been a particular hero ever since he burst onto the scene with a great golf game and an ability and willingness to make the game fun for spectators. It was hardly surprising that he wanted to be honoured with a par-3 hole near water in view of the fact that one's letter reached him not long after he had won $1-million for a hole-in-one at such a hole! So, it had to be the sixth hole for Trevino as a stream runs tight along the left edge of the green .

It was imperative that a hole be named in honour of Tony Jacklin. Some people tend to forget his role in raising European golf to the levels it has enjoyed in the last thirty years. He set the place alight when winning the (British) Open at Lytham in 1969, the first home winner since Max Faulkner in 1951, and following up with a victory in the US Open in 1970.

There was nobody he feared at that time and he could have won three more Opens. He was on a birdie blitz at St. Andrews when a thunderstorm halted play in 1970; he was third in 1971; and he was deprived of the 1972 title at Muirfield only by Lee Trevino's multiple chip-ins including the famous holed chip at the seventy-first hole! Nobody had such bad luck until Greg Norman's sequence of near misses years later.

When one visited Jacklin in his home in Jersey at the end of the 1970s he expressed severe disenchantment with the Ryder Cup. Ironically, he was to be invited to be team captain soon after that and he played a huge role in transforming the event into a classic.

He set new standards and goals for the European players, insisting that they be treated first-class and think first-class, and the rest is history. We named hole thirteen for him.

Old Tom Morris wasn't around when one got started so a little liberty was taken in naming the first hole for him. He was, after all, the man who really started the modern game. When great champions like Johnny Miller and Tiger Woods visited us we honoured them as well.

So far, sixteen champions have been honoured with holes named for them. The list reads:-

1. Old Tom Morris	2. To be named.	3. Tiger Woods	4. Sam Snead
5. Peter Thomson	6. Lee Trevino	7. Arnold Palmer	7a. To be named.
8. Fred Daly	9. To be named.	10. Jack Nicklaus	11. Gary Player
12. Billy Casper	12a. To be named.	13. Tony Jacklin	14. Gene Sarazen
15. Henry Cotton	16. Johnny Miller	17. Tom Watson	18. Byron Nelson

HEROES AT HOME

The amazing loyalty of Jimmy O'Toole

While seeking to maintain and strengthen connections with internationally recognised friends in golf it was most important that thought should be given to one's old friends at home also as work got underway on the establishment of The European Club.

Just how significant and strong many of those friendships have been is best illustrated with a story concerning the indescribable generosity of the late Jimmy O'Toole and his wife Carrie.

Here was a man who loved his golf and loved people. He was a member at the Castle Golf Club and was one of the driving forces behind the Leinster Golfers' Alliance which has spent decades promoting the interests of junior golf in the area. He played decently off a single figure handicap.

We had been friends for years and there could be no other choice of architect for the clubhouse. He loved everything about the project and could not have been more helpful in everyway even to the extent of arriving down from Dublin with son Vincent to volunteer for grass cutting duties!

There could have been no other choice for Club Captain and he was astounded when invited to take-up that office for life! He was delighted at the offer of captaincy but, being a modest fellow, took a little persuading on the unheard of concept of captaincy for life.

One's argument was that it is disruptive and unnecessary to change club captain every year when one has a perfect man holding office and the basic sense of this was duly accepted.

Great plans were prepared for the clubhouse. It was a time of dreams. For example, one had a fancy for an indoor putting-green surrounded by a pond. While waiting for food to be served a golfer could hit a few putts or even chip over the water! But when it got to doing the job common-sense prevailed

102

Jimmy O'Toole, far right, was the first captain of The European Club and he is seen here strolling the links in the early days with his friend Pat Ruddy. O'Toole and his wife Carrie presented a bronze model of the club's dolmen logo to the club with the base serving as a unique combined President's Board, Captain's Board and lasting record of the winners of the major club events. Seen above with the dolmen are, from left, Fintan Russell Jnr., Jimmy O'Toole, Bernardine Ruddy and the club's second captain Fintan Russell.

and one decided that work should proceed in three or more phases to spread the costs and match the demand for facilities.

O'Toole had completed recently the clubhouse for St. Margaret's Golf Club near Dublin Airport, where the course had been designed by oneself and Tom Craddock, and it was lovely. He was even more sure-footed at Brittas Bay as he matched form and function with precision and, above all, made the wisest choices in the matter of external finishes which would require very little maintenance despite being located in a hostile environment near the sea.

He was, however, very concerned for the well-being of the project and simply astounded my wife Bernardine and I when he and Carrie sought a meeting one sunday morning in the cabins we were using as a temporary clubhouse while the permanent structure was being built nearby.

"Look,' he said, 'Carrie and I had a meeting last night and decided that we would remortgage our home and give most of the proceeds on interest-free loan to you so that you can build more of the clubhouse now. It will never be cheaper than it is now to build," he argued as he concluded by stressing that Carrie and he wanted nothing in return for such generosity. He wanted nothing except to see his friend getting on with the job and succeeding.

Such an offer was astounding. It would be astounding even within a family. It was flattering. It was humbling. It could not be accepted. But it proved once more that here was a king amongst men and that Carrie was a queen! One stuck with the phased plan approach and enjoyed playing golf together in the years leading-up to his death. His memory lives on. The base of the wee dolmen which Carrie and he prepared for the club serves as our honours board, listing the club's officers and the winners of major events, and it is hoped that it will be a dignified monument to them for centuries.

Phase 2 of the clubhouse was undertaken in 2005 when a golf shop, reception area and office were added beyond an arched hallway between it and Phase 1 which contains changing-rooms and a dining area and lounge. That hallway has proven itself a big winner as players like to congregate there when preparing to go out in wet or blustery conditions. It also provides a direct line of travel between the eighteenth green and the car-park without having to find one's way around a wide building. It all works well.

Phase 3 has been planned as an apartment and office space upstairs. This will afford facilities to have private gatherings with special friends when they call. It will also provide comfortable quarters from which to direct day-to-day operations and write a little about golf.

104

A fun concept will see the inclusion of a balcony from which golf balls can be chipped onto the eighteenth green or driven back up the eighteenth fairway. This is hardly as extravagant an idea as it may seem as the green and fairway are already in existence and there is never anyone on that hole until almost midday and most golfers are gone long before dusk.

To rise in the morning to the view of the golf course and to sit in the lounge watching the shadows crawl across the links as the sun goes down are keenly anticipated pleasures.

The most eagerly anticipated element is the library, which will also be known as the golf-writers' room, to house the approximately 3,000 golf books one has collected since my brother Fintan started it all back in 1961 by giving one a present of Eric Brown's autobiography "Knave of Clubs." That book was enjoyed greatly and has been a treasured possession ever since.

It was golf-writing, and golf photography, which opened the world for people before the advent of television and one has always had a reverence for the profession and for those who ply it. It has always been a thrill to write about golf and try to convey some of the excitement of the sport to others. It seems only right that part of The European Club should be dedicated to one's fellow professionals.

The idea is to have the books, one of the largest collections in the world and growing apace, safely housed along with the many thousands of golf pictures one has taken over the years. At some stage, it would be good to employ some young people to write summaries of the books and cross-reference them to enhance their value as a research resource. Then, visiting golf-writers could relax while working and even fit-in a few holes of golf to relieve the tedium.

Otherwise there is no particular rush to enlarge the clubhouse as the plan is to keep it fairly intimate and elegant in a simple way. Its function is to give shelter, to provide solid golfers' food, to afford the player an opportunity to buy a glove or a ball and to give clean and warm changing facilities. It should not be ostentatious or be allowed to grow to the point where it is a financial burden.

Speaking of finance reminds one to write about our second captain for life, Fintan Russell. Here is another special man who has been a benign and helpful influence since we met way back when in Castlebar Golf Club. He was a bank manager in those days and he proved wonderfully trusting and supportive when one's first effort at building a golf course was made in the 1970s. Whenever there was a need for financial advice he was the man to call. So, when we needed a new captain he was the man to call once more.

Sport fairly courses through his veins as his father, Paul, was one of Ireland's all-time great footballers with County Kerry and Fintan's personality is relaxed and gregarious. Unfortunately, he did not work-out his life term as captain and chose to retire from office when reorganising his home to Oughterard. He remains a trusted confidant.

Our third captain is another winner in the person of Eddie Fallon. Again, friendship has existed between us for many decades and his love for the game had led him into captaincy of the Leinster Alliance, into being the first director of golf at The K-Club and into presidency of the Irish Golf Secretaries' Association before we invited him to be our captain.

Fallon's temperament is ideally suited to the position. He is virtually unflappable. He never misses a beat when it comes to protocol and diplomacy but he remains alert to all things which need doing and he has a charming ability to make everyone feel most important.

Simplicity is the best formula in organising a golf club. When starting The European Club one had the opportunity to observe what has worked and has not worked for thousands of other clubs which had been formed before it and to, as it were, avoid some of the obvious pitfalls.

It seemed to one that most clubs had too many members leading to difficulties in gaining tee-times. It was resolved that we would never fall into that trap. Our highest level of membership to date has been 130 and so it is possible to get a game pretty close to the required time while the links is very, very quiet for prolonged periods and people can enjoy an uncrowded game or fiddle about on their own trying to work-out a swing thought or two.

Some clubs place too great an emphasis on competitions, one felt, to the extent that one might feel unwelcome at one's own club unless willing to enter the event of the day. So, it is that we have one competition weekly and that is on sunday mornings. Otherwise, members make-up their own games. It seemed to one that clubs had developed a habit of rolling golf into a social-business-sporting package and de-emphasising the golf course and the golf. It was resolved to keep a total focus on golf.

It seemed to one that clubs had a habit of spending large sums of money on things that didn't really need doing, especially on those huge clubhouses which were seldom fully used, and so made the game more expensive than necessary. So it was resolved that there would be no rush to excess grandeur other than making every effort to gain a perfect and uncrowded links.

It seemed to one that there was an excess of politics at most clubs. So we resolved to have a captain for life and a president for life and a minimum of officers besides. After all, golf is a simple pursuit and its organisation at club level doesn't really require endless meetings.

It was decided that the club would have a Senate comprised of people who were one's trusted friends of many years' standing and that they would have the right to make suggestions but with no power to enforce them! Their wisdom and friendly presence was all that was required.

Sadly, five of the original Senators have died. But the others look healthy enough at time of writing and should be around for years to come.

Pat Coyne turned-out to be the most active of the Senators. Our fathers had been friends and we had got along well together since our first meeting in the late-1950s. He has played for Connacht and competed in the various amateur championships in six decades! He is as keen a golfer as any on this planet and he spends endless hours on the practice tee searching for the perfect golf swing. His favourite spot out there has been named Coyne's Corner.

Jim Harnett, who has grown old enough to have been captain at Portmarnock, has always made himself available to bounce ideas off and his accountancy skills are trusted utterly. It is interesting to note that a number of our other Senators have become the captains of their other clubs ..... Loyal Goulding at Cork, Pat Hynes at Skerries, Dermot Melia at Howth, David O'Neill at Killarney and Richard Reid at Forrest Little ..... so they must be pretty astute.

Paul Mulcahy, a man of great optimism and ideas, has had a lifetime association with golf thanks in no small part to his uncle Jack who founded the modern Waterville Golf Club; Brian Morgan has a worldwide reputation as a great golf photographer and he always views life positively through the lens or otherwise; George Kimball is a global traveller with a valuable global view of things and it was quite an honour being asked to be his bestman at a lovely New York wedding where George Foreman performed the ceremony for Marge and George; and Joe Cowhie and Hugo Flinn always make a visit to Druids Glen a pleasure and their brave way of playing the shot has been a lesson.

The other members of the original Senate, all of whom remain treasured friends after twenty years of The European Club, are - boyhood hero Harry Horan, Brian O'Brien-Kenney who was one's solicitor when he had a practice of his own, photographer Charles Briscoe-Knight, Ciaran Lynch, Michael MacCaughey, Paddy Murphy, Larry O'Brien and Jack O'Leary.

There will be additions to the Senate membership from time-to-time as the years go by. It is a good idea to have a group of clear-headed lovers of the game willing to discuss elements of club organisation as it evolves. Normally, of course, there will be little to discuss and a major requirement for gaining and holding office will be an ability to look good in sandals and toga!

TESTED BY CHAMPIONS

Championships at eight venues test design skills.

It was a totally different golfing world when work commenced on establishing the links of The European Club. Metal woods, for want of a better description, were just beginning to gain acceptance and persimmon was on the way out. The new "hot" golf balls were just emerging.

It was about then, too, that laser measuring devices became readily available and replaced the chain and the metre wheel to make life infinitely more pleasant for those of us engaged in the planning of golf courses. Now it was possible to secure rapid and accurate measurements in all visible directions. For example the length of the shot being planned and the safety distance between it and the next hole could be established exactly and rapidly without having to walk about. Without having to work!

Television, too, was playing its part in transforming the world for golf architects as the statisticians fed viewers with information on the play of the champions. Heretofore, one had to go to championships and make notes of the shotmaking abilities of the players. Now, the television started to feed us a mine of information such as driving distance, distance remaining, wind direction and strength as standard nightly fare. Better still, they did it for men and women, old and young.

It was an exciting moment in golf architecture and it was fortuitous that it coincided with the making of our links. Any earlier golf course had to become dated right then and there with costly and highly disruptive changes required to get back in line with the modern game.

Aware of where the world was going, and armed with more information than had been available ever before in the history of the game, one set about establishing a golf links which would standup to the modern players and equipment. One also provided for the next fifty years to avoid early obsolesence. Of course, those setting-up the links for daily or for championship play do not have to use the entire design feature arsenal when doing so. There needs to be an intelligent interplay between the designer and the course manager. An over aggressive manager, using all the back-tees no matter what and

The most powerful fourball played at The European Club consisted of Tiger Woods, David Duval when he was about to defend his Open title, Mark O'Meara and Scott McCarron. Tiger set a course record 67. Bernardine and Pat Ruddy made all four honorary members.

hiding the pins behind hazards, can destroy a designer's reputation. On the other hand, intelligent management will see the design being played like a grand piano by making correct allowance for prevailing weather conditions and the expected standard of play. The mission at The European Club, and at any other place that one designed for championship play, has been to create a vast multiplicity of options for mixing and matching power and finesse in the set-up of the course of the day.

Happily, one has lived to see twenty-one championships played on eight courses that one has designed or at places, Donegal and Portsalon, where one has carried-out extensive enough modernisation and redesign to claim a design interest or ownership. Allowing that championship week can be turbulent, the outcome has been satisfying. This is a list of "my" championships, with the line-up of champions:-

1994 -	Irish Ladies' Open Championship at St. Margaret's	Laura Davies
1996-	Murphys Irish Open Championship at Druids Glen	Colin Montgomerie
1997-	Murphys Irish Open Championship at Druids Glen	Colin Montgomerie
1997-	AIB Irish Seniors' Open Championship at St. Margaret's	Tommy Horton
1998-	Murphys Irish Open Championship at Druids Glen	David Carter
1998-	Irish Ladies' Open Championship at Ballyliffin	Sophie Gustafson
1999-	Murphys Irish Open Championship at Druids Glen	Sergio Garcia
2001-	Irish Ladies' Amateur Close Championship at The European Club	Alison Coffey
2002-	Northwest Ireland Professional Open at Ballyliffin	Adam Mednick
2002-	Severiano Ballesteros Trophy at Druids Glen	Team event
2003-	Irish Ladies' Amateur Close Championship at Donegal	Martina Gillen
2004-	Irish Men's Amateur Close Championship at Donegal	Brian McElhinney
2004-	Irish Professional Close Championship at St. Margaret's	Padraig Harrington
2004-	Montreal Open Professional Championship at Montreal Island	Stephen Woodard
2005-	Irish Ladies' Amateur Close Championship at Portsalon	Patricia Mangan
2005-	Montreal Open Professional Championship at Montreal Island	Peter Tomasulo
2006-	Irish Professional Close Championship at Druids Heath	David Mortimer
2006-	Irish Ladies' Amateur Close Championship at The European Club	Patricia Mangan
2006-	Irish Men's Amateur Close Championship at The European Club	Rory McIlroy
2007-	Leinster Youths' Open Championship at The European Club	
2007-	Irish Professional Close Championship at The European Club	

The 2001 Irish Ladies' Amateur Championship was won by Alison Coffey, right, from Claire Coughlan, left. The great champions Philomena Garvey and Mary McKenna, who had won the title fifteen and eight times respectively, presented a picture on behalf of the I.L.G.U. to The European Club captains Carol Haugh and Fintan Russell. The gathering included Elaine Bradshaw, club president Pat Ruddy and I.L.G.U. president Cathy Smith.

HOSTING NATIONAL CHAMPIONSHIPS

The ultimate honour of hosting national events

The ultimate honour available to any golf place is to be invited to play host to the national championships. To be officially recognised as good enough by the national governing bodies of golf is an affirmation of achievement. That is how one viewed it when the Irish Ladies' Golf Union allowed us host the Irish Ladies' Amateur Championship in 2001 and in 2006; when the Golfing Union of Ireland allowed us to host the Irish Men's Amateur Championship in 2006; and the Professional Golfers' Association gave us the privilige of hosting the Irish Professional Championship in 2007.

A most interesting pattern emerged over the course of the amateur championships as, in each and every case, the defending champion emerged victorious! Obviously our links is very suited to the play of champions.

In 2001, the Irish Ladies' Championship was played in glorious weather and with a great deal of nostalgia in the air as Mary McKenna, eight times winner of the title between 1969 and 1989, came out of retirement to underline our friendship and show the young girls a little bit of her wizardry by surviving a few rounds. Her presence was much appreciated and very historic and it was equally thrilling to see her predecessor as Queen of Irish golf Philomena Garvey at the presentation. It is rarely that one gets to see these two great champions together and it was marvellous that it happened at The European Club.

The final was fought-out between two Curtis Cup players with Alison Coffey holding onto her title despite the best efforts of Claire Coughlan.

112

Championship winner Patricia Mangan prepares to cut the victory cake after the Irish Ladies' Close Championship 2006. In attendance, from left, club president Pat Ruddy, the I.L.G.U. president Ann Heskin, sponsor Helen Feeley, runner-up Martina Gillen and lady captain Carol Haugh.

The weather was not so obliging when the ladies returned in 2006. In fact, it was a terrible week with rain, storms and fog taking turns to disrupt play. The combination of wind and low-mown greens produced problems during the final when the ball tended to move on the putting surfaces and it was only the quick thinking of referee Bridget McCaw which saved the day as she ordered that the greens be watered when the final match was two or three holes away!

It was another all-Curtis Cup final, it cannot get better than that in Irish ladies' golf, as Patricia Mangan managed to withstand the power game of Martina Gillen. A second double was involved this time as Mangan had won on another Pat Ruddy designed links at Portsalon the previous year.

There was great excitement during the week due to the presence of the Maguire twins, Lisa and Leona, at age eleven! They justified themselves when both made it into the matchplay stage.

It was championship time again within a matter of weeks as the Irish Men's Amateur Close Championship took place with another teenage wonder taking centre stage in the person of defending champion Rory McIlroy who had just passed his seventeenth birthday and was soon to be elevated to the No. 1 Amateur Golfer in the World.

The links was set-up tough for the championship with narrow fairways and tall rough. The rain stayed away but the wind blew. In fact, it blew most of the competitors away but not young McIlroy who started his first qualifying round at the tenth and was three-under-par after nine holes with Tiger Woods' links record of 67 well within his reach. He didn't make it. But a 70 left him in cruise gear for the second round.

He continued to play superbly confident, aggressive golf all week and there was never going to be another winner. He played as if there was no rough as he powered his drives straight and true and eventually overcame Simon Ward in the final.

The championship activity continued into 2007 with the Leinster Youth' Open, which always gives an early look at boys soon to be big names as amateur golf becomes increasingly dominated by the very young, and the Irish Professional Championship scheduled for the early weeks of July. The plan with the latter event was to give Padraig Harrington a good warm-up on links for the (British) Open at Carnoustie the following week. It is unusual for an old fellow to describe a much younger man as one of his heroes but that is the way one views Padraig Harrington. Ireland is hopeful that he will win a major one day. He fell just a shot short of a playoff at Muirfield in 2002 having practiced and mentally conditioned himself at The European Club the week before with his late dad's help.

Rory McIlroy receives the trophy from G.U.I. vice-president Thomas Basquille after winning the Irish Amateur Close Championship 2006. Assisting at the presentation, from left: Union general secretary Seamus Smith, Union honorary secretary Albert Lee, club captain Eddie Fallon, club presidents Bernardine and Pat Ruddy, sponsor Simon Russell, head greenkeeper Gerry Arthur and Leinster G.U.I. chairman Barry Doyle.

IRISH LADIES' AMATEUR CLOSE CHAMPIONSHIP 2001

Played at The European Club on June 27 - July 1, 2001.   Sponsored by Lancome.

Qualifying Scores -

150   Alison Coffey (Warrenpoint) 78, 72.

151 Elaine Dowdall (Wexford) 75, 76.

153   Helen Jones (Strabane) 81, 82.

154   Eileen Power (Kilkenny) 76, 78.

155   Martina Gillen (Beaverstown) 77, 78; Patricia Mangan (Ennis) 76, 79.

156   Claire Coughlan (Cork) 80, 76.

157   Jennifer Gannon (Co. Louth) 80,77.

158   Suzanne Corcoran (Portumna) 78, 80.

159   Hazel Kavanagh (Grange) 79, 80.

160   Paula Delaney (Co. Louth) 81, 79; Mary McKenna (Donabate) 79, 81;
Therese O'Reilly (Grange) 78, 82.

162   Sue Phillips (Woodbrook) 82, 80.

163   Naoimh Quigg (City of Derry) 80, 83.

164   Valerie Hassett (Ennis) 80, 84; Deirdre Smith (Co. Louth) 79, 85.   165   Una Marsden (Tullamore) 84, 81.

166   Michelle Carroll (Grange) 83, 83; Mary Sheehy (Tralee) 80, 86.

167   Marian Riordan (Tipperary) 86, 81; Darragh McGowan (Ballybofey & Stranorlar) 83, 84.

169   Bridget Gleeson Healy (Killarney) 84, 85; Maura Morrin (Curragh) 84, 85; Eileen MacMullen (Donegal) 84, 85;
Maria Dunne (Skerries) 83, 86.

170   Pat Doran (Donabate) 86, 84; Joanne Black (Knock) 86, 84; Mary Dowling (New Ross) 82, 88;
Sheena O'Brien-Kenney (Grange) 82, 88; Anne Geoghegan (Athlone) 81, 89.

172   Susan Mullaney (Co. Louth) 85, 87; Michelle Holmes (Enniscrone) 83, 89.

MATCHPLAY:

First Round - Coffey beat Holmes, 19th hole; Marsden beat Smith, 6 and 5; Corcoran beat MacMullen, 1up; Gannon beat Dunne, 5 and 4; Dowling beat Gillen, 1up; McKenna beat McGowan, 3 and 2; O'Reilly beat Riordan, 3 and 2; Power beat Kenney, 5 and 4; Jones beat Geoghegan, 3 and 2; Phillips beat Sheehy, 1up; Healy beat Delaney, 5 and 4; Black beat Mangan, 2 and 1; Coughlan beat Doran, 6 and 5; Kavanagh bt Morrin, 1up; Quigg beat Carroll, 1up; Dowdall beat Mullaney, 6 and 5.

Round of Last- 16- Coffey beat Marsden, 4 and 3; Gannon beat Corcoran, 3 and 2; Dowling beat McKenna, 19th; Power beat O'Reilly, 6 and 5; Phillips beat Jones, 19th; Black beat Healy, 2 and 1; Coughlan beat Kavanagh, 4 and 3; Dowdall beat Quigg, 2 and 1.

Quarter-finals- Coffey beat Gannon, 3 and 2; Dowling beat Power, 1 hole; Black beat Phillips, 5 and 4; Coughlan beat Dowdall, 1 hole.

Semi-finals- Coffey beat Dowling, 4 and 3; Coughlan beat Black, 4 and 3.

Final- Coffey beat Coughlan, 4 and 3.

IRISH LADIES' AMATEUR CLOSE CHAMPIONSHIP 2006

Played at The European Club on May 13-17, 2006.   Sponsored by Lancome.

Qualifying Scores -

153   Patricia Mangan (Ennis) 80, 73; Mary Dowling (New Ross) 80, 73; Martina Gillen (Beaverstown) 73, 80.

155   Sinead O'Sullivan (Galway) 77,78.   159   Deirdre Smith (Co. Louth) 79, 80.

162   Marian Riordan (Tipperary) 79, 83; Maura Morrin (Curragh) 79, 83; Sinead Keane (Curragh) 78, 84.

164   Jennifer Gannon (Co. Louth) 81, 83; Danielle McVeigh (Royal County Down Ladies) 80, 84.

165   Maria Dunne (Skerries), 84, 81; Gillian O'Leary (Cork) 78, 87.

166   Darragh McGowan (Ballybofey & Stranorlar) 85, 81; Claire Coughlan (Cork) 80, 86.

167   Victoria Bradshaw (Bangor) 83, 84; Fiona Carroll (Athenry) 77, 90.   168   Deirdre Walsh (Milltown) 84, 84.

169   Lisa Maguire (Castle Hume) 79, 90   170   Dawn Conaty (Ashbourne) 85, 85.

171   Sarah Faller (Galway) 88, 83; Holli Snelling (Killarney) 85, 86.

173   Suzanne Phillips (Woodbrook) 86, 87.   175   Vicki Power (Brampton Park) 81, 94.

177   Sarah Cunningham (Ennis) 88, 89; Sheena O'Brien Kenney (Grange) 87, 90; Leona Maguire
      (Castle Hume) 87, 90.

178   Linda Toomey (Limerick) 90, 88; Joanne Black (Knock) 88, 90.   179 Sandra Atkinson (Woodbrook) 85, 94.

180   Ann Marie Dalton (Coollattin) 92, 88; Miriam Abernethy (Cork) 89, 91; Louise Mernagh (Woodenbridge) 84, 96.

MATCHPLAY:

First Round -   Mangan beat Mernagh, 6 and 5; Carroll beat Walsh, 1-hole; Gannon beat Cunningham, 4 and 3; Kenney beat Keane, 3 and 2; Smith beat Black, at 19th; O'Leary beat Snelling, 1-hole; McGowan beat Faller, 1-hole; O'Sullivan beat Atkinson, 4 and 3; Gillen beat Dalton, 7 and 6; Coughlan beat Conaty, at 20th; Dunne beat Phillips, 1-hole; Riordan beat Toomey, 3 and 2; Morrin beat Leona Maguire, 3 and 2; McVeigh beat Power, 7 and 6; Bradshaw beat Lisa Maguire, 1-hole; Dowling beat Abernethy, 5 and 4.

Round of Last-16 - Mangan beat Carroll, 2 and 1; Gannon beat Kenney, 7 and 6; Smith beat O'Leary, 1-hole;   McGowan beat O'Sullivan, 3 and 2; Gillen beat Coughlan, 1-hole; Dunne beat Riordan, 3 and 2; McVeigh beat Morrin, 1-hole; Bradshaw beat Dowling, 2 and 1.

Quarter-finals-

Mangan beat Gannon, 2 and 1;   Smith bt McGowan, 2 and 1; Gillen bt Dunne, 2-holes; McVeigh bt Bradshaw, 8 and 6.

Semi-finals -   Mangan beat Smith, 1-hole; Gillen beat McVeigh, 3 and 2.

Final -   Mangan beat Gillen, 2 and 1.

IRISH MEN'S AMATEUR CLOSE CHAMPIONSHIP 2006

Played at The European Club on June 10-14, 2006.   Sponsored by Golfsure.

Qualifying Scores -

150- A Pitcher (The Island) 75 75, R McIlroy (Holywood) 70 80

151- S Lowry (Esker Hills) 77 74, S Ward (Co Louth) 73 78

152- D Morgan (Mullingar) 75 77

154- S Power (West Waterford) 80 74, K O'Neill (Strandhill) 80 74, A McCormick (Scrabo) 78 76, E O'Sullivan (Island) 74 80, J Turner (Royal Portrush) 72 82, A Morrow (Portmarnock) 70 84

155- W McCully (Donaghadee) 79 76, J Caldwell (Clandeboye) 72 83

156- N Turner (Muskerry) 81 75, C Curley (Newlands) 78 78, P Sheehan (Ballybunion) 78 78, D Crowe (Dunmurry) 75 81, N O Briain (Royal Dublin) 74 82

157- D McInerney (Lahinch) 77 80, K Stack (Dungarvan/UCC) 76 81, G Bowden (Hermitage) 75 82, A McCloy (Ballymena) 75 82, D O'Brien (L'town & B'town) 72 85

158- C McNamara (Limerick) 80 78, F Rafferty (Dungannon) 73 85

159- D Finn (Mallow) 81 78, D Rawluk (The Island) 80 79, R Leonard (Banbridge) 77 82, A McAllister (Portmarnock) 77 82, P O'Kane (Moyola Park) 76 83, G Lawlor (Citywest) 76 83, N Gorey (Killeen) 75 84

160- P Sheehy (Limerick) 80 80, P Murray (Limerick) 78 82, B O'Connor (Hermitage) 76 84, M Sinclair (Knock) 75 85

161- R Boal (Scrabo) 81 80, A Glynn (Porters Park) 81 80, S Grant (Birr) 79 82, A McKinley (Shandon Park) 78 83, R Cannon (L'town & B'town) 76 85

162- S Crowe (Dunmurry) 81 81, J Hughes (Douglas) 81 81, C McAleavey (Banbridge) 79 83, P O'Hanlon (Curragh) 79 83, C Doran (Banbridge) 78 84, S Dwyer (Newlands) 78 84

163- J Somers (L'town & B'town) 83 80

164- D Lewis (Woodbrook) 84 80, D Coyne (Tuam) 82 82, E McCormack (Galway) 82 82, D Moran (The Island) 81 83, K Lewis (Skerries) 78 86, N Grant (Knock) 77 87, H Diamond (Holywood) 77 87, R O'Connor (The Island) 77 87

165- M King (Athenry) 86 79, B McCarroll (Ballyliffin) 82 83, S Loftus (Ennis) 81 84, C Daly (Castletroy) 81 84, J Toner (Woodbrook) 80 85, M Campbell (Stackstown) 80 85, A O'Callaghan (Douglas) 79 86, R McCarthy (Island) 79 86.

MATCHPLAY:

First Round -
Caldwell beat Dwyer, 4 and 3; Lawlor beat Lewis, 2-holes; Coyne beat Boal, 2 and 1; N. Turner beat Somers, at 19th; Doran beat Diamond, 3 and 2; McCloy beat Hughes, 5 and 4; Gorey beat O'Neill, 4 and 2; McNamara beat J. Turner, 3 and 2; Cannon beat McCarroll, 2-holes; Stack beat O'Brien, 3 and 1; Daly beat Moran, 1-hole; D. Crowe beat McCarthy, 2 and 1; Pitcher beat S. Crowe, 2 and 1; Sheehy beat Campbell, 4 and 3; S. Grant beat McKinley, 1-hole; McIlroy beat Morrow, 2 and 1; N. Grant beat Power, 3 and 2; R. O'Connor beat McAleavey, 2-holes; McInerney beat Loftus, 3 and 2; Ward beat K. Lewis, 7 and 6; Finn beat McAllister, 5 and 4; King beat B. O'Connor, 2-holes; Sinclair beat McCormack, 4 and 3; Toner beat Lowry, at 19th; Leonard beat Bowden, 3 and 2; O'Kane beat Curley, 2-holes; Glynn beat Sheehan, 2 and 1; Morgan beat O'Callaghan, 1-hole; O'Hanlon beat McCormick, 2 and 1; O'Briain beat O'Sullivan, 1-hole; Rafferty beat McCully, 6 and 4; Rawluk beat Murray, 20th.

Second Round -
Caldwell beat Lawlor, 4 and 3; Coyne beat Turner, 1-hole; Doran beat McCloy, 5 and 4; McNamara beat Gorey, 2 and 1; Cannon beat Stack, 3 and 2; Crowe beat Daly, 1-hole; Pitcher beat Sheehy, 5 and 4; McIlroy beat S. Grant, 5 and 4; N. Grant beat O'Connor, 1-hole; Ward beat McInerney, 1-hole; Finn beat King, 1-hole; Sinclair beat Toner, 3 and 1; O'Kane beat Leonard, 4 and 3; Morgan beat Glynn, 5 and 3; O'Hanlon beat O'Briain, 1-hole; Rafferty beat Rawluk, 3 and 2.

Round of Last-16 -
Caldwell beat Coyne, 6 and 4; Doran beat McNamara, 6 and 5; Crowe beat Cannon, 3 and 2; McIlroy beat Pitcher, 6 and 5; Ward beat N. Grant, 1-hole; Finn bt Sinclair, 1-hole; O'Kane bt Morgan, 3 and 2; Rafferty bt O'Hanlon, 2 and 1.

Quarter-finals -
Doran beat Caldwell, 2 and 1; McIlroy beat Crowe, 1-hole; Ward beat Finn, 6 and 5; O'Kane beat Rafferty, at 19th.

Semi-finals -   McIlroy beat Doran, 2 and 1; Ward beat O'Kane, 2 and 1.

Final-   McIlroy beat Ward, 3 and 2

The Final Score

Developing a golf place of one's own has seen a lifetime ambition fulfilled.

Having one's wife and children alongside throughout the project has knocked the lonely edge
off the trek so thanks to the two Bernardines, Gerard, the hard-working
twins Patrick and Sidon, and Zilla.

Seeing the grandchildren arrive and reach for golf clubs is astounding and rewarding and the hope
is that the place will give pleasure and pride to Andrew, Poppy, Lilla
and to any others who come along to join the party.

The work continues to make The European Club as fine and happy a golfing place as possible.
To be recognised amongst the finest golf courses in the world is a massive honour
and beyond the wildest imagination of a young boy back in the west of Ireland
and dreaming of great golfers and great places in the post-War 1950s.

Bernardine and I have trodden the sands together, seen grass grow and now enjoy the fairway.
Hopefully, those who visit with us will have a happy experience. That is our wish.